Ronald E. Day: Foundational Writings

Ronald E. Day: Foundational Writings

Library Juice Press
Sacramento, CA

Copyright 2024

Published in 2024 by Library Juice Press.

Litwin Books
PO Box 188784
Sacramento, CA 95818

http://litwinbooks.com/

This book is printed on acid-free paper.

Publisher's Cataloging in Publication
Names: Day, Ronald E.
Title: Foundational writings / Ron Day.
Description: Sacramento, CA : Library Juice Press, 2024. | Includes bibliographical references.
Identifiers: LCCN 2024950076 | ISBN 9781634001755 (acid-free paper)
Subjects: LCSH: Information science – Philosophy. | Information science – Political aspects. |
Information theory. | Critical theory. | Phenomenology. | Poetics.
Classification: LCC Z665.D39 2024 | DDC 142.7--dc23
LC record available at https://lccn.loc.gov/2024950076

Contents

1	**Introduction**
17	**Classification, Systems, and the Time of Metaphor**
59	**Animal Songs** Translation, Community, The Question of the 'Animal': In-formation
111	**Index**

*To Michael Buckland,
who said to me about "Animal Songs" that
"there should be more like this," and then
aided me so that there could be.*

Introduction

This book contains two works written while I was a Master of Library and Information Studies student at the School of Library and Information Studies at the University of California, Berkeley (UC Berkeley) during 1992 ("Classification and the Time of Metaphor") and 1993 ("Animal Songs"). Three years previously I had earned a Ph.D. in Comparative Literature in a track interdisciplinary with Philosophy, from the State University of New York at Binghamton. The works at Berkeley were written for a cultural heritage class with Professor Michael Buckland and a tutorial with then Emeritus Professor Patrick Wilson ("Animal Songs" for both) and for an introductory class on Knowledge Organization with Professor Ray Larson ("Classification and the Time of Metaphor"). A third text, a shortened form of "Animal Songs," was published online in a short-lived journal titled *Standpoints* in 1996, edited by Kathleen Burnett, but it is not included in this book. The two works included here have been only lightly edited for typographical and bibliographic errors. I'd like to thank Sommer Browning for her careful copyediting of these works and Rory Litwin for publishing these works.

At the time these works were written, as is the case with many programs still today, Library and Information Science (LIS) units were focused upon library, and more generally "information," professional education at the master's level, and upon more computationally intensive education at the doctoral level. Concerns with the social or cultural power of information and with the history of information science other than regarding libraries were not central foci for such programs or research in the field.

Michael Buckland's concerns with the conceptual meaning of the term "information" and his work in the history of Library and Information Science were exceptions. Historical figures like Paul Otlet and Suzanne Briet were European and wrote in French, and they didn't seem to have much to do with librarianship per se or the world of computational information. In the 1990s, Buckland, W. Boyd Rayward, Robert

Williams, Trudi Bellardo Hahn, and others did the hard work of establishing these historical figures and others as "pioneers" of information science in the professional society of the American Society for Information Science (ASIS; now, Association for Information Science and Technology (ASIS&T)).

While a student in the introductory Reference course of the school, my teacher, Marcella Genz, recommended that we should read Michael Buckland's book, *Information and Information Systems* (Buckland, 1991a). (A condensed version of some of the theoretical parts of this book is given in Buckland's article, "Information as Thing" (Buckland, 1991b).) Such a professionally oriented book, albeit of "theory" in LIS, wasn't the type of book that I regularly read at the time. (I was reading post-structuralist influenced works and Wittgenstein's philosophy). But I did find its trilogy of "information-as-knowledge," "information-as-process," and "information-as-thing" to be interesting, though I read this as a phenomenology of information, rather than as definitions of information. (In a recent article (R.E Day, 2024) I have given an updated version of this reading.)

"Animal Songs" was a further gloss on this phenomenological reading of Buckland's categories, though read through post-structuralist and philosophical sources, especially the works of Martin Heidegger and Gilles Deleuze. Essentially, the essay argues that information-as-process leads to information-as-knowledge and this becomes information-as-thing when information is understood as an epistemic substance, this last being the latest historical form of what Martin Heidegger and Jacques Derrida called the "metaphysics of presence." (One could, of course, read this critique through Karl Marx's theory of the commodity, as well.) This, what I would later call the modern conception of information (R. E. Day, 2001), requires that the materiality and history of the process of arriving at and asserting information is erased in the assumption that information is some sort of found, "auto-affective" datum (that is, going back to the Latin roots of the term "data," something self-given). (The concept of "auto-affective" means that the entity makes itself present without other mediation.) A few years later in *The Modern Invention of Information* (2001, the title was borrowed from Armand Mattelart's book, *The Invention of Communication*), I would argue that the historiography of information in popular information age discourses was also based on the erasure of previous information ages, so that each information age has been seen as new and revolutionary. In these works, I argued that "information," in the sense of auto-affective presence, has been a premier modernist trope. That is, shorthand for asserting a whole cultural and social apparatus for forms of epistemic presence as the "new." This trope would, as we now know, spur speculative investment, creating the dot com economic bubble on the back of "information society" and "information age" hoopla, and in the field of LIS it would be the rhetorical mechanism for the "i-school movement" to assert itself as a transformational moment in society and education.

Other influences in "Animal Songs," beyond Buckland's work, will be clear to the reader. Namely, Heidegger's philosophical works and post-structuralist works of the time, the former which I began reading as an undergraduate and the latter as a graduate student and even more so after receiving my Ph.D. Avital Ronell's *The Telephone Book: Technology, Schizophrenia, Electric Speech* (Ronell, 1989) was an important influence on this essay, as well. Ronell's was one of the first books that engaged in a critical theory reading of technology, and it opened up a path for me. At the time, only "computer professionals" seemed, in academe and beyond (e.g., Computer Professionals for Social Responsibility (CPSR)), to be privileged to critique information technology within a social context. Ronell's book engaged, in a Heideggerian and Derridean fashion, the ontological foundations of "electronic" technologies. And typographically, the book performed a graphic critique of the central transfer metaphor in most ordinary theories of information and communication, the "conduit metaphor." Ronell's work introduced a cultural critique that had social power.

I was already familiar with the 19th and 20th century "conduit metaphor" (Reddy, 1979) for communication and information through the work of the Language poet, Barrett Watten's, "Conduit" (Watten, 1988). It is no coincidence that many of the most "critical" writers in LIS during a generation were involved in critical poetics and small press production earlier in their lives. Prominent among these have been Johanna Drucker, Sandra Braman, and more recently, Wayne de Fremery. Drucker's early works were as a Language poet, as well as a printer, graphic artist, and publisher; my own Comparative Literature Ph.D. dissertation was on Language Poetry/Language Writing and I had briefly worked after college for the printing offshoot of Station Hill Press, Open Studio Print Shop, printing English translations of Maurice Blanchot's books, among others; Fremery's Ph.D. is on Korean poetry and he had worked with his family's small press publishing venture; Braman was a poet and co-publisher, with her husband the fiction writer Douglas Woolf, of Wolf Run Books. And there have been a few other people in LIS and in the library profession who were active when they were younger in the small press and poetics movements of the San Francisco Bay Area.

We shouldn't be surprised at this relationship between critical poetics and critical information studies, since the critique of information is the critique of the sociotechnical formulation, distribution, and use of language (and for Drucker, graphics and images). In the past 50 years we have seen, from the whitewashing of language under Reagan, to Bush I and II, and now Trump and company, the effects of the sociotechnical media manipulation of language upon politics and daily life. This was the target of the Language Poetry/Language Writing movement, and it is, or at least should be, a central concern in critical information studies.

It is worth adding in this regard that George Lakoff, the noted UC Berkeley cognitive scientist, linguist, specialist on the topic of metaphor, and sometime political commentator, was interested in Language Poetry in the Bay Area. And Ronell had personal friendships extending into the poetics and publishing avant-garde in San Francisco. Also, like many others in these circles, at the time of writing the essays in this book I had just recently spent quite a bit of time reading the later Wittgenstein, and earlier, after college, reading translations of Russian symbolists, futurists, and formalists, the texts of which had only recently begun to appear in translation through Ardis Publishing during the 1970s. In sum, the critical understanding of language and its limits and possibilities for politics were very much in the air, from international and national politics to (in the case of New Narrative) the micropolitics of gender and sexual relations.

When I was a student at UC Berkeley, and thereafter when attending meetings of the American Society for Information Science and the Association for Library and Information Science Education (ALISE), I was amazed that so few people seemed interested in the historical and discursive aspects of information. Where students couldn't see any topics to write on in the field, all I saw was topics! My sense at the time was that the field lacked a vocabulary for such discussion with any depth. The "science" of information science and the practical emphasis in library science were acting as impediments to other interesting work that could be done in the discipline.

Before summarizing the two papers in this collection, I would like to acknowledge two of my teachers that these pieces were written for. Michael Buckland's reaction to "Animal Songs" was "more should be done like this." Michael was kind to encourage and mentor me. Through it all, he has been a great teacher and friend.

The late Ray Larson's remark on "Classification and the Time of Metaphor" was "fascinating," written on the top of my returned paper. From Larson, an information scientist whose research was on information retrieval, I learned about the Classification Research Group and the Macy Conferences on Cybernetics, the latter which would lead me to Norbert Wiener's work and the chapter in *The Modern Invention of Information* (2001) discussing this history. Ray was a gentle, kind, and humanities-educated person. From his work on the Cheshire information retrieval system for libraries, I also learned a bit about the algorithmic weighting of data, which would later allow me to gain an appreciation for neural networks in AI.

It is interesting that the information "user" or "seeker" has been conceptualized as such an autonomous element in LIS research, where in more computationally oriented information science—from Claude E. Shannon's information theory to cybernetics to today's machine learning—the user is conceived as a statistical function. On the one hand this autonomy is an admirable product of the library and documentation tradition, but on the other hand it is a residue of the conduit metaphor and the metaphysical tradition, so that this autonomy is taken as absolute, that is, in terms of metaphysical subjectivity. It is important to recognize information theory in the sense that Shannon offered it, that is, statistical, for understanding the "positioning" (a central term in my book *Indexing It All* (2014)) of persons as "users" by sociotechnical systems and algorithms. Cybernetics has never ended. If I argued that the concept of the "user" was dead (R.E. Day, 2011b), it was only so that we could better understand persons and selves in relation to documentary and information systems. The theoretical reification of selves and persons by the concept of the "user" (or equally, the "seeker" of information) merely replicates the similar abstraction of documents by the concept of "information." We need to understand more about the technical nature of different information systems in sociocultural contexts in order to understand how they shape information out of documents and users out of people.

Though the critique of "Animal Songs" and my first book, *The Modern Invention of Information: Discourse, History, and Power* was upon the understanding of information as epistemic substance, these works did so in order to open the concept of information to an older notion of information (as being informed of something) and especially in the first of these works, to a broad notion of affect along these same lines. However, there were no attempts in these works to argue that the critique should lead to a social science. Their application to "positive" projects in the social science is complex. These critiques could only be formulated philosophically.

A Summary of "Animal Songs"

The first part of "Animal Songs," the introduction, introjects the concept of "translation," as a marker of difference in language, into the modern conception of information as auto-affective meaning. "Information," understood as auto-affective, in Otlet's term, a "fact," is an instance of the metaphysical understanding of entities as self-caused and simply given. The modern conception of information, from Otlet through the information age's conception of information, involves the erasure of the material and historical construction of information (Day, 2001). Such a conception was later epitomized by the notion of "raw data." Information has been, thus, the latest trope for what Derrida called "metaphysical presence."

The second part of the essay deals with the information society, understood at the time as a neoliberalist, seamless and smooth flow of language and exchange. It ends, however, with fears regarding the emergence of fascism from this goal of seamless flow. Informational capitalism, as a cybernetics of standardized flows of language and eventually being, is seen as an inversion of fascism. After neoliberalism's information economy disrupts localized communities by supposed universal flows, fascism returns to assert this totality in a more "pure," nationalist or racial, form. In both these cases, community as emergence is left behind in visions of community as a whole and as a totality.

In contrast to the previous section, the third part develops the notion of singularity, arising from an immanent multiplicity within both selfhood and community. "Singularity" here emerges from the potential powers of entities expressed as shaped, that is as afforded, by their environments. Within human society, this means other people, as well as cultural forms such as language and traditions. Singularity is contrasted with individuality, which is seen in the liberal political tradition as folded within the state (and in fascism as forming it through identification). Walter Benjamin's notion of "language as such," as the potentiality (or in this same sense, the "virtuality" of language) of meaning, is one means for the emergence of a community of difference not based on individuality but on singularity. (This chapter foreshadows later works on community (R. E. Day, 2004) and engagements with the works of Antonio Negri and others of the Italian autonomous movements (R. E. Day, 2002, 2011a, 2011c), the latter which I was introduced to when I was a visiting faculty member at the University of Oklahoma from 1999-2001, thanks to Timothy S. Murphy.)

In this third part of "Animal Songs" there is also introduced the concept of "in-formation," particularly in relation to non-human animals. The concept of in-formation (sometimes signified more explicitly as "in-(>)formation" in this paper), was meant to signify information as a *relation* and as a *becoming* of language and affect to some ideational, identifying, form. As a being, we are always already in a relation with others, always already becoming to the beings that we singularly are, but only through differential relations out of common properties. With non-human "animals" this difference is more marked than between humans but, like with other humans, it occurs through the in-common properties of finitude, extension, affect, and language. Contrary to Wittgenstein's statement in *Philosophical Investigations* that "If a lion could talk, we couldn't understand him," I would assert that lions do talk and sometimes we do understand them. "Language," understood as in-common affects, is the basis for a shared community expanded to the scale of all living beings. As brought out in Jean-Luc Nancy's essay, "Beheaded Sun" (Nancy, 1989) (referenced in "Animal Songs"), there is no other authentic identity than the infinite splitting and sharing of those in-common properties. In short, being is emergent through its in-formational relationships based on those properties. Information, understood as a substance, is the reification of in-forming processes.

The fourth part explores more the space of the "in-between" of entities. Such relations run before and after the entities involved, in terms of their experiential and bodily potentialities, both separately and in common. "In-(>)formation" signifies this interspace of mutual becoming, of mutual ontogenesis, upon the "planes" (Deleuze, 1987) of shared properties and individual and collective potentialities. It is an event of in-formation rather than an entity taken as "information," either in the sense of a documentary form or as epistemic substance.

"Animal Songs" ends with a summary that argues for studying the particular and singular in information (a theme that I returned to in my book *Documentarity* (2019)), though at the time of "Animal Songs" it referred to a time when one could feel abandoned by all political and theological salvation, an abandonment by, at the time of the essay's composition, universal flows of information, capitalist driven globalism, and neoliberalism. This was a period before the attention economy of the internet; it was a time when one could feel alone and be alone. Here, information will not save us, but rather our attention, our listening to, the relations of others, within in-formation. This is a vision of information as ontological and epistemic *différance*: not something seemingly present and always distant, but something distant but always present, both to us and within us. Not liberal difference, and certainly not "conservative" or today's and yesterday's far-right community/nationalism, but rather Being that is always already to arrive, because it always already is here, through the shared possibilities of extension, finitude, affect, and language.

A Summary of "Classification and the Time of Metaphor"

As noted above, "Classification and the Time of Metaphor" was written during my first semester, fall 1992, in the Master of Library and Information Studies program. This class covered cataloging and searching, the latter done through paper bibliographies and by command line Dialog, LexisNexis, and online library catalog searching. Ray Larson taught the class and in it he mentioned the British Classification Research Group, whose publications I then found in microfilm at the University's main library, and he mentioned the Josiah Macy Jr. Foundation conferences in cybernetics during the 1950s. I was fascinated by the concept and history of library and information "systems" and what "systems" meant in this context. I was also fascinated by the natural philosophy metaphors that I was seeing in the literature on bibliography and libraries.

For one of the Dialog assignments in the class, I looked up "post-structuralism" and ran across the works of Robert Cooper in organizational studies in England. Cooper's work is mentioned and cited in this essay. Bob was interested in post-structural understandings of systems theory too, and a few years later he very generously invited me to Keele

University's Center for the Social Studies of Technology (CSST), which he headed, despite my being only a middle and high school librarian at the time. ("I don't care what you do; what matters is that your work is interesting," he so very kindly told me.) (Coincidently again, in terms of information science and poetics, Robert Cooper was much earlier the real-life figure, unfortunately cruelly depicted, in my former, beloved, teacher, Robert Creeley's, autobiographical 1963 novel, *The Island* (Cooper, 2016).) As a guest at Keele's CSST, I met Steve Brown, Martin Parker, and others working in organizational studies, critical accounting, and psychology—overall at the time, in "Critical Management Studies"—all using post-structuralist and Marxist approaches (so very unlike what was going on in these fields in American universities). The work of these scholars, very pointedly critical of the neoliberal and "empirical" takeover of their professional areas and academic departments, echoed my skepticism regarding the ostrich-like and sometimes explicitly hostile reaction of LIS to any consideration of critical thought in the "library schools" and professional organizations of the time. Their example later led to my (subverted) attempt to establish a functioning Special Interest Group in critical information studies at American Society for Information Science.

One question that led me to writing "Classification and the Time of Metaphor," which remains for me today, was why it took so long for zoological classification structures from the 18th century to influence library classification structures of the mid-19th century, particularly in terms of their universal application. (The late Francis Miksa at the University of Texas once commented to me during a conference that it was because a universal classification was not yet needed in libraries, as they were not large enough, but I suspect there's more to it.) In addition, I was interested in this paper in metaphorical drift and analogy within scientific disciplines and also between the social sciences and natural sciences. (It was only in the later 2000s that I would return to the works of my one-time professor at the State University of New York at Binghamton, the brilliant and prolific Oxford philosopher Rom Harré, and gradually find help in understanding this last issue.)

"Classification and the Time of Metaphor," starts in "Chapter one" with trying to understand the drift of natural science metaphors and classificatory systems epistemology into library science. (I am pleased to note that independently Wayne de Fremery in his book *Cats, Carpenters, and Accounting: Bibliographical Foundations of Information Science* (Fremery, 2024), has recently provided a fuller historical and theoretical account of this problem.) "Chapter two" of the paper examines the temporality of information systems in terms of what Heidegger called the vulgar or everyday understanding of temporality based on the concept of time as durational presence: the now and its successive moments. Against such temporality is the temporality of human psychology (such as Freud's notion of deferred affects and historical revision vis-à-vis memory—*Nachträglichkeit*) and Heidegger's concept of repetition (*Wiederholung*). Information systems have the properties of both asserting a presence and also tying those presences into flows, both as durational series of now and as the anticipated temporal presence of such (and thus, desire and addiction appear—for example, with internet web surfing and internet addiction).

It is important to mention in this last regard that when "Classification and the Time of Metaphor" was written the graphic user interface World Wide Web (WWW; that is, the usable graphic, not command line, format for the "internet" as we now know it) had not yet appeared. However, this paper touched upon issues that became important with the WWW, such as the internet's development as a medium for commodity exchange, internet addiction, and the fragmentation of community through the internet.

Subsequent Works

If these two papers were "foundational works," then how have they influenced my subsequent works?

A summary of parts of "Animal Songs" appeared in my first book, *The Modern Invention of Information: Discourse, History, and Power* in 2001. The critique of the conduit metaphor was continued in a paper on this theme (R. E. Day, 2000). Analyses of humans and other beings as powerful particulars, and community as expression from powerful particulars and sociocultural-technical relations, have continued in one form or another throughout my works. (In such works, I have relied upon Deleuzian expressionist philosophy, works by Antonio Negri and other members of Italian *Autonomia*, and more recently Rom Harré's analyses of powerful particulars across different ontological types.) Sometimes my articles on these topics explicitly engaged political discourses (2002, 2011a, 2011c). An expressionist philosophy of information regarding ontological types and within the context of evidence understood representationally was most completely put forth in my 2019 book *Documentarity* (R. E. Day, 2019). Social affects, understood as social capital, were explored in my critiques of Knowledge Management in the early 2000s. And the theme of information as differential affects in documentation systems and "in-formation" as affective attunements continues with my current work. Systems theory was reengaged in terms of a critique of LIS's concept of users (R. E. Day, 2011b, 2014). And a critique of informational tropes in the documentation, library, and information science traditions of the 20th century and in the information society and information age rhetoric at the turn of the 21st century was investigated in *The Modern Invention of Information* (2001), as well as in articles and interviews of that period. Information technologies are fundamentally rhetorical in nature, technologizing sociocultural expressions and communication, and so my works have always been implicitly or explicitly related to problems of rhetoric.

My current work (to be published in a book by MIT Press), interprets neo-documentalist works (works by Michael Buckland, Bernd Frohmann, and earlier, Robert Pagès) through Martin Heidegger's early hermeneutic phenomenology and his later examination of natural beings (*phusis*—physics, nature) as powerful particulars. This develops the theme of the powerful particular in the form of "animals" that was in "Animal Songs" and can be found in the figure of the antelope in Suzanne Briet's 1951 book, *Qu'est-ce que la documentation?* (which I co-translated into English in 2006). The forthcoming MIT Press book will also more fully develop the notion of "in-formation" in "Animal Songs" as a phenomenological becoming of what is evidential. The central issue here is that of reference, epistemology understood as an issue of ontology. With the advent of the Document Academy conferences in the late 1990s, thanks to Niels Windfeld Lund and Michael Buckland, and readings of Bruno Latour's works, I've come to a better appreciation of how documentary processes afford knowledge of the evidential powers of animals. While "Animal Songs" and "Classification and the Time of Metaphor" belong to a negative critique of information as metaphysical presence, I've increasingly come to appreciate the role that documentation has in providing the "gathering" or "collection" (as Heidegger put it) where the powers of living beings can be understood as knowledge, in addition to mutual sense relations. In other words, my phenomenological understanding of in-formation has increased as I've better understood that such is based on both natural powerful particulars and epistemic documentation processes. This present book and the forthcoming MIT Press book may be read, respectively, as the beginning and conclusion of the deconstruction of the modern conception of information.

I should mention that Neal Thomas's brilliant works, particularly his book *Becoming-Social in a Networked Age* (Thomas, 2018) has been a major help to me in understanding newer digital systems over the past ten years. And Michael Buckland's original historical recoveries, critical thought, and dialogue with me continue to be resources and inspiration. Also, I should point to at least one major misreading or lack of reading in my early works that can only count as a lost opportunity, and that is of the works of Bruno Latour. Latour was, in some ways, the ultimate theorist of documentality, though one attuned to the technologies and practices of the natural sciences. I have come to a better understanding of Latour's works rather late. Though later is better than never, the lateness is a pity.

I have always seen my work as the beginning of a larger project, that of bringing critique into an otherwise narrowly empirical or pseudo-empirical field. The stakes of not doing so are too high, since we are well-aware from the distant, and now also the recent, past of politics that "information" is not something fixed, but interpreted, and through human communication and information management, produced. The historical, cultural, social, technological, and economic means for this—that is, the "material" means—must be made clear. Yet in LIS, so much of master level education remains focused on doing and so much of doctoral level research remains that of literature reviews and rather mechanical empirical studies whose intellectual importance is unclear. With the glittering term of "information" still in vogue (sometimes now "data"), the information schools continue a technical and a social informatics influenced agenda of researching information technologies in society (along with many other departments and schools) and the professional organizations dedicate themselves to the vague goal of investigating and serving the relation between "people and technology" (when did people not use technology? And which technologies?). And as for knowledge? In information science and informatics (but not in library, archives, and museum studies, of course) the basis for knowledge now seems a sometimes neglected or forgotten element in the discourse of "information," despite the historical repetition of attacks on knowledge institutions by far-right political actors.

Interestingly, of late the profession of librarianship has seen some of the most interesting conceptual advances, with critical librarianship in some forms and with "whole person" librarianship. Confusion remains, however, between accepting a liberal conception of the public within a vastly unequal system for speech, access, and other goods, and pushing for a public that can be, and must always be, fought for. Between fantasized "free speech" and responsible and knowledgeable speech, and between traditional library systems beholden to restrictive copyright and so-called "shadow" libraries. Many of these confusions seem to arise from ideological beliefs within the library profession itself and the limits that practical professionalism puts upon critical thought.

The purpose of writing "Animal Songs" and "Classification and the Time of Metaphor" was to punch open a hole in the discourse of the field of Library and Information Science, to create a possibility for thinking in what at that time was impossible. The publication of these works is not just personal and retrospective, but as in all my works the intent is to suggest what is still possible, if not in the particular, at least as a model of trying to express what still lays distant, not only in research, but in society. Each work has been part of a broader, longer project. I recognize that the discursive style and the references, particularly in "Animal Songs," are several decades old and that many of the issues discussed in these works have been addressed (though perhaps in unexpected and even problematic ways) in the intervening years in the LIS fields. But I believe that the project set out in these works is still in progress, and so I hope that their publication may prove not only of historical, but perhaps, contemporary interest and use. The politics espoused in these works is still to emerge, the relation to non-human animals is still to come, the valuing of the common properties of beings has in some ways been in retreat. In short, our lives are bound together through in-common "animal songs" that in-form us as the beings that we are and are bound to be.

Since the space "in-between," the space of animal songs, the in-formational space between not only humans, but humans and non-human beings, and in a Heideggerian fashion, between Being and beings, is given by the fact of language, the reality of finitude and physical extension, and the community of affect, the realization of knowledge and being from what is in-common is possible. Fundamentally, if not always in practice, empirical science is based on such commonalities, and from such we hope to form knowledge, as validated understandings of what the world is. We are informed of and by things and this forms the relationships of our being. (To be is to be always related; it is to be through others, and therefore be-with (Heidegger: *Mitsein*), from the past into the future, and therefore to also be present-with other beings.) Thus, the projects of these papers still hold the promise of that which is to appear, because the grounds are always there, even when the singularities from this univocity are then individualized, divided, commodified, and in general reified and broken into divisions of tastes and identities, by capitalist and metaphysical subjectivation. We need to always "reengineer" information back into its in-formational relations, just as we need to understand individuals in terms of their becomings. In-formation is animal songs. Our attunements to these animal songs, our turnings both toward and away from them, both as a concept and in their instances, events, and systems, requires skills of attentive listening and not just hearing. So, too, in reading these pieces, I hope the reader will bring an attentive listening, an active imagination, and not too quick a judgment.

There's no substitute for reading, especially an index.

Bibliography

Buckland, M. K. *Information and Information Systems*. Praeger, 1991a.

Buckland, M. K. "Information as Thing." *Journal of the American Society for Information Science*, 42(5), 1991b. 351–60.

Cooper, R. *For Robert Cooper*. Eds. G. Burrell & M. Parker. Routledge, 2016.

Day, R. E. "The "Conduit Metaphor" and the Nature and Politics of Information Studies." *Journal of the Association for Information Science and Technology*, 5(1), 2000. 805–11.

Day, R. E. *The Modern Invention of Information Discourse, History, and Power*. Southern Illinois University Press, 2001.

Day, R. E. "Social Capital, Value, and Measure: Antonio Negri's Challenge to Capitalism." *Journal of the American Society for Information Science and Technology*, 53(12), 2002. 1074–82.

Day, R. E. "Community as Event." *Library Trends*, 52(3), 2004. 408–26.

Day, R. E. "The Aleatory Encounter and the Common Name: Reading Negri Reading Althusser." *Journal of Communication Inquiry*, (35), 2011a. 362–69.

Day, R. E. "Death of the User: Reconceptualizing Subjects, Objects, and Their Relations." *Journal of the American Society for Information Science and Technology*, 62(1), 2011b. 78–88.

Day, R. E. "From Advocates to Terrorists: Ideology, the State of Exception and State of Emergency, and Political Ethics." *Journal of Information Ethics*, 20(2), 2011c. 65–84.

Day, R. E. *Indexing it All: The Subject in the Age of Documentation, Information, and Data.* MIT Press, 2014.

Day, R. E. *Documentarity: Evidence, Ontology, and Inscription.* MIT Press, 2019.

Day, R. E. "Documentation to Documentality in the Works of Michael Buckland." *Journal of Documentation*, 8(3), 2024. 606–13.

Deleuze, G. & F. Guattari. *A Thousand Plateaus.* Trans. B. Massumi. University of Minnesota Press, 1987.

Fremery, W. d. *Cats, Carpenters, and Accountants: Bibliographical Foundations of Information Science.* MIT Press, 2024.

Nancy, J.-L. "Beheaded Sun (*Soleil cou coupé*)." Trans. B. Gold & B. Holmes. *Qui Parle*, 3(2), Fall 1989.

Reddy, M. J. "The Conduit Metaphor: A Case of Frame Conflict in Our Language About Language." *Metaphor and Thought.* Ed. A. Ortony. Cambridge University Press, 1979. 284–310.

Ronell, A. *The Telephone Book: Technology, Schizophrenia, Electric Speech.* University of Nebraska Press, 1989.

Thomas, N. *Becoming-Social in a Networked Age.* Routledge, 2018.

Watten, B. *Conduit.* GAZ, 1988.

Classification, Systems, and the Time of Metaphor

Abstract

The purpose of this paper is to explore classification theory and systems theory from the aspect of knowledge and information, especially in regard to bibliography. This paper discusses fundamental concepts in information from an historical and philosophical perspective.

This paper is concerned with the play of metaphor within, and as, classification schemata and systemic structures, and the problems of vocabulary transfer and vocabulary stabilization in discourses of "classification," "knowledge," "systems," and "information." This paper is also concerned with the temporality of systems and the ways in which this temporality interfaces with human desire to form cybernetic functions.

This study aims to ask, what are the critical horizons for classification, systems, and information (understood systemically) within the Western metaphysical tradition?

Chapter 1 The Metaphors of Classification

Library and information literature often leave traces of another origin. Consider this passage from the preface to Michael Buckland's *Information and Information Systems*, an introductory text that seems to partly aim toward a philosophy of information from the side of information science. As our first quote, it will be extensive:

> This book originated in 1980 when I sought to clarify for my own benefit the nature of the affinity among different examples of retrieval based information systems. I hoped to develop a comparative anatomy of species of information systems. The initial result,

however, was a fairly detailed analysis of the anatomy of one species only, undertaken as a preliminary case study: *Library Services in Theory and Context* (1983; 2nd ed. 1988). The broader, more ambitious goal reemerged in 1988... the idea that museums ought to be included in the family of information systems. Museums are not normally viewed as information systems, but they select, collect, store, and retrieve items expected to be informative. They behave like information systems.... I have tended to concentrate on exotic and complex examples because they seemed to me to be not only more interesting but also more useful for the purpose of developing robust ideas about the nature of information systems. Moving from one species, libraries, to the whole family of information systems...

(Buckland, xiv)

The question of how the "nature" of knowledge moves from a classificatory *episteme* to a systemic one, is no simple matter. Particularly when "nature" itself is invoked, in all its schematizations, to speak of knowledge, though it is knowledge that will, in the end, speak of nature. This circle of hermeneutics, a circle of *episteme* and *phusis* [physics/nature], is well-known since Aristotle, and so too, as Heidegger reminds us, is it forgotten during the Western metaphysical and scientific tradition's progression.[1] It is a forgetting which, framing philosophy and science, "enframes" (Heidegger, *Gestell*) the matter of their inquiry. I do not wish to carry Heidegger's modernist protest against "technology" itself into this paper for many reasons, not the least being that at this juncture "technology" denotes a wide range of functions for machines, and also because the factual cybernetic relations human beings have with technology have far outstripped both humanist protests for a return to 'the human' as well as arguments that machines are 'mere tools,' or, 'simply machines.'[2] But it is this forgetfulness that we often find throughout the literature on classification and systemics, and it is this forgetfulness which, I would argue, we must remember if we are to disentangle vocabularies of "knowledge," "classification," "systemics," and "information" in ways other than clumsy attempts at definition.

Buckland's metaphorical taxonomy ("nature," "families," "species," "exotic," etc.) is not alone in the literature of bibliography or information since the 19th century (see the appendix of this paper for taxonomic and sun metaphors within bibliography).ᴬ Throughout library and information literature, natural metaphors abound. The prevalence of metaphor in scientific 'fields,' however, is generally denied. Metaphor disrupts the definitiveness of discursive 'fields'; it threatens their status as 'scientific discourse.' Metaphor cuts through the boundaries between fields so much so that the division between 'knower' and 'object' itself can rupture. Such accepted divisions as that between natural and artificial classification and between human and machine can become blurred in their sharing of theoretical models, temporalities, and vocabularies. The second chapter of this paper will argue the essential metaphoricity of systems; in this chapter I am concerned with metaphor within, and as, classification, as knowledge poses as classification from the late Renaissance through the 18th, 19th, and even into the 20th centuries. This is a period during which the epistemic distance intrinsic to medieval allegory fades, and positivism dreams of the collapse of Knowledge and Nature in scientific law.

As W. C. Berwick Sayers and others argued, classification schemata of knowledge have a tradition reaching back to Aristotle, to the medieval trivium and quadrivium, to Bacon's three-fold philosophical/psychological classification schemata (which predates Kant's three-fold division of reason), to modern "universes" of classification where subject areas take the place of "genus" and books the place of "species."[3] In his *Manual of Classification*, Sayers even argues the theological foundations of classification, attributing classification to God, and consequently, (bibliographic) order to nature.[4][5] It is with the 18th and the 19th centuries, however, that discourses of nature and knowledge begin to correspond, first with knowledge dreaming of the ability of knowledge to know the entire universe of beings down to the most microscopic entity, and then with knowledge dreaming of its own classification, too (Ranganathan's "universe of knowledge" (Ranganathan, *Philosophy*, chapter 4), or as Sayers writes: "What is the material of classification? The answer is everything." (Sayers, 26)).[6][7] The completeness that

---

A Author's note, 2024: The appendix of the original paper has been removed for this publication because of copyright and reproduction issues. It consisted of several diagrams from published documentation, archival, and library sources, showing biological metaphors for knowledge organization in these fields, largely based on species-genus relationships. "Classification and the Time of Metaphor" asked the question of why library science literatures borrow their metaphors so heavily from biological classification. For a more contemporary and deeper explanation of this themes, see Fremery's (2024) recent analysis.

18th, 19th, and 20th century classification schemata aim toward is a total one, following organic metaphors of being, from the microscopic to the macroscopic, from the atomic 'part' to the universe as a whole.

The organic metaphors of classification theory result in, and are a result of, its overall re-presentational structure. From static conceptions of the universe (such as Leibnitz's reflexive monads and medieval figurations of a static hierarchical universe) to 19th century evolution and system theories, knowledge and nature mirror each other in Law. As Hegel and other Idealist philosophers recognized, repetition and representation are only possible as a thing is understood in terms of an already true self-presentation. The law of repetition not only informs the morphological structures of classification and systems, but also, as metaphor, runs through and constitutes the totality of the sciences. As R. C. Paton and others have argued, "metaphors have a creative function in science," (Paton, 282) which can be measured not only through the expansion of metaphorical paradigms from one field into the next, but by showing the bounds of science 'itself' as it is constituted by repetitive 'fields.'[8]

It is important to remember, however, that metaphorical repetition rests on an already present consistency of scale; otherwise, metonymy occurs and the two discourses stand in tension in relation to one another.[9] The organic metaphors of classification schemata are thus symptomatic of more original structures, closer to the hermeneutic circle. As Foucault has noted in regard to the historical construction of natural systems in the late 18th century, whether universal classification schemata are understood according to a "system" of differences or according to a "method" of exclusive classes or species:

> Both system and method rest upon the same epistemological base. It can be defined briefly by saying that, in Classical terms, a knowledge of empirical individuals can be acquired only from the continuous, ordered, and universal tabulation of all possible differences.... From the seventeenth century, there can no longer be any signs except in the analysis of representations according to identities and differences. That is, all designation must be accomplished by means of a certain relation to other possible designations. To know what properly appertains to one individual is to have before one the classification—or the possibility of classifying—all others. Identity and what marks it are defined by the differences that remain.
>
> (Foucault, 144)

This play between identity and difference within classification schemata already rests upon a potentially complete classification, which in turn rests upon the belief that nature can indeed be represented and that it can be best represented in a reflexive, representational structure of parts in a totality.

Because of his preeminent position and influence in the area of library classification, because he is one of the last of the great bibliographic classifiers, and because metaphysical and epistemological assumptions are foregrounded in his writings, the writings of the famous Indian librarian S. R. Ranganathan are useful to examine in the context of this paper. As Ranganathan notes, classification is not concerned with the "entities themselves" but rather with their representations (*Philosophy*, 96). The quickness by which this warning is forgotten and the quickness by which knowledge and nature collapse, however, can readily be understood by Ranganathan's notion of the "universe of knowledge."

Maybe one of the most interesting examples of the representational constructions of classification is provided by Ranganathan in part 682 of his *Prolegomena to Library Classification*. There we find a "metaphysical analogy" to the "universe of knowledge," where Ranganathan derives from an organic metaphysical universe an organic bibliographical universe:

Soul (Universal)	=	Universe of knowledge
Individual soul	=	Class of knowledge or subject Equation of Document

Applying the analogy to the universe of books, we get the following correspondences:

Soul	=	Thought-content
Subtle body	=	Language or other medium and form of exposition
Soul + Subtle body	=	Work
Gross body	=	Material in which work is embodied
Soul + Subtle body + Gross body	=	Document

(*Prolegomena*, 384)

Classification schemata need a concept such as the "universe of knowledge" so that descriptive knowledge can occur for the findings of science or for the future subjects of books within that schema. Conversely, because of the assumption of a complete (and universal) knowledge, it is first and foremost assumed that a classification scheme *should* be able to encompass beings whether known or unknown. Lovejoy describes the 18th and 19th century's search for the "missing link" between humans (with reason) and so-called 'animals' ('without reason,' symbolized by apes). This search was carried out in both science and popular culture in order to fulfill "necessary conditions of plentitude" within a universe of God's infinite (yet, paradoxically, substantive) being.[10] As Lovejoy notes, these searches for missing parts within the Law of nature were carried out with much zeal, especially where empirical gaps were thought to be 'found' or where the 'lowest,' often microscopic forms of life were thought to lie 'hidden' from God-inspired human knowledge (Lovejoy, 233 ff.). As Henry Louis Gates Jr. notes in a slightly different context, the violence of racism is founded on such notions of 'types' which result from a certainty of totality and representational knowledge. One can read in the works of such philosophers as David Hume, Immanuel Kant, and G. W. F. Hegel how 'Black' Africans were, in the 18th and 19th centuries, typed as a 'missing link' between European reason and 'animals' (Gates, 10). The violence of division into identities is possible only if a scale is fixed through such a notion as a 'classification' or a 'system'—otherwise, as Foucault noted, an economy for identification could not exist, and 'types' could not be.

Derived from the imperative of the "universe of knowledge," Ranganathan's "canon of Hospitality" in colon classification is based on this notion of potential knowledge:

> Hospitality in Chain
>
> We now pass on to the enunciation of the second special canon to be observed in the construction and use of a scheme of classification of the Universe of Knowledge, as a result of the universe consisting of an infinity of entities some of which are now unknown and may become known only in the future.
>
> (*Philosophy*, 106)

Ranganathan notes earlier, in the *Philosophy of Library Classification*, that a failure to provide for "hospitality" in the construction of a classification "chain" will result in a scheme of classification that will "cease to be a scheme and will land itself in chaos." The success of this play between the order of the scheme as a totality and its hospitality to new entities or 'parts' both marks the dramatic success of the scheme and it also verifies that values outside that scheme will stay excluded. The forgetting that an order can only be (that is, as a presence) through the repression of all that exceeds its boundaries is intrinsic to the success of such an order—that is, as support for its internal claims of truth. The pressing need for such a presence, for a substantive Being of being, however, is itself symptomatic of the inability of the system to be self-defining. This framing, however, is precisely what is denied (or 'forgotten') when the nature of system reflects the system of nature within the hermeneutic circle.

Within Ranganathan's faceted classification the category "personality" plays a pivotal role in subject classification. It is an interesting category because it denotes the essential Being of a being (much as the medieval category of "esse" or the Greek "*ousia*"), and thus centrally grounds the faceted schema in representation. That classification schemata depend on objects understood as re-presented (and not that the language game of a schema or system constructs the being for that object) is essential for the exclusive truth claims that classification schemata and systems make.

Representation occurs, too, in the 'transmission' of knowledge. Ranganathan's bibliographical "analogy," above, suggests containment metaphors for language, which themselves are a precondition for a "conduit" metaphor for understanding or 'communication.'[11] In Ranganathan's language, "thought content" ("the soul") is contained or embodied in symbols (as the soul is embodied in the physical body). This Platonic understanding of language is repeated in modern texts on information theory and it manages to mask how meaning is constructed in schemata and systems through a series of differences within a privileged frame.[12] Once thought is embodied in symbols (i.e., 'words'), then language is said to 'transport' meaning over space and time as if it were a conduit for the symbol's signified meaning. What is important here is that meaning's produced frame is forgotten and is replaced by a symbolism that is devoid of space, time, and power. The conduit metaphor cannot explain hermeneutic difficulties in language, it cannot explain non-representational discourses, it cannot explain 'non-communicative' functions for language; in sum, the conduit metaphor cannot explain the hermeneutic and social constructions of meaning. Because the conduit model is grounded in representation, structural claims as to the "situational" (Buckland, 50) nature of "knowledge" or "information" come into immediate conflict with the transcendental claims of representation. In much the same manner, Jacques Derrida in *Of Grammatology* has argued that 'the father of structural linguistics,' Ferdinand de Saussure, in his *Course in General Linguistics* remained bound within representation even while arguing that language constructs meaning through a play of differences.

The significance of understanding language as a neutral medium *for meaning*, instead of as a construction which *gives meaning*, is that, first, it obscures problems of resistance and undecidability by language (say in poetics), and second, it defines all meaning by assumptions of closed systems of understanding and "communication." The resultant privileging of discourses (e.g., 'scientific' vs. 'aesthetic') is obvious. What isn't so obvious is that such a theory understands time and space as ethereal mediums that play no functions in the construction of meaning. What is important is not only the absolute violation of hermeneutic and social functions in the construction of meaning, but the annulment of time and space as values for meaning. In the conduit metaphor, time and space only play a role in the construction of meaning by the total (re-)presence of meaning that appears at each end of the conduit line, in the total voice, the total word, or the total text. Otherwise, space and time are ethereal at best or, at worse, lead to 'delay' of transmission.

The transportation value of a value-free language, however, is interesting to note. Ranganathan, for example, sees libraries as institutions devoted to the representation of meaning. Because of the explicitness of many of the assumptions I have been discussing, I will quote from it at length:

> Apart from the aesthetic joy which individuals may derive from its pursuit, library classification is essentially a product of social forces. That is because the library itself is a social institution charged with a set of social duties. These duties center on one social purpose. That purpose is the activation of the human mind by the transmission of thought-energy across both time and space. Thought-energy gets created in the human mind and it is best transmitted through the whole personality of the one whose mind it gets created [through that person's "immediate presence"] …. But society is spread out far wider in time and space…. Alternative ways have

therefore to be used, though they are less effective, even as we are obliged to use preserved, powdered milk when fresh milk is not available. One of the alternative ways is to transform thought-energy into a material, portable form which can be preserved for any length of time and transported across any distance. By preservation of the material, it can be made to reach posterity and posterity can re-transform it into thought-energy and get its own mind activated by it.

(*Philosophy*, 77)

Just as Buckland argues that knowledge is the intangible of which information is the tangible representation of, for Ranganathan, the "presence" of 'thought' or idea (*eidos*), formerly guaranteed by a person, is preserved in the "material" of writing; a preservation which then can be reconstituted and consumed by another person. Here, the metaphysical/metaphorical tradition of knowledge as substance, eating another's knowledge, eating one's own words, food for thought, etc., is given in all its sacrificial and cannibalistic gore (save only, perhaps, that Ranganathan's Hindu background prevents us from asking for the 'meat of the matter' or 'where's the beef?').[13]

But the metaphysical tradition of which Ranganathan's text is so obviously a symptom is evident, also, in modern texts on information and systems theory. Citing Mooers ("Information Retrieval Viewed as Temporal Signaling"), Buckland confirms that information retrieval is "communication through time" (Buckland, 61).[14] Though Buckland argues that this definition "is a little frayed," it is not for reasons of the conduit metaphor. Instead, time is understood as a somewhat resistant medium by which delay occurs. "Delay" thus accounts for the presence of time in information systems, and in fact, is said to be an "attribute of all communication and of all uses of information-as-thing..." (Buckland, 61). In the next chapter, we will investigate the notion of delay as intrinsic to the presence of a certain notion of time. At this point, however, it is enough to simply confirm that the function of time for both classification and systems theory is the same: namely to appear as the ethereal conduit for the presentation and re-presentation of fully constituted meaning.

For Ranganathan there is a humanist good in the 'consumption' of knowledge over space and time, because through such a consumption, from the most "macroscopic masses of thought embodied in books to microscopic units of thought embodied in articles" (*Philosophy*, 84), the universe of knowledge is engulfed, as it were, "democratically" (*Philosophy*, chapter 3), piece by piece.[15] (One wonders if the final result of such consumption on the largest possible scale would not be, as in Hegel, the historical end of an Idea, that is, a form of knowledge.) For information theory, the result of becoming informed is, initially, not so universal (save in such prophecies as H. G. Wells' "World Brain" (cited in Robins and Webster, 68)), but is a change of mental state in the receiving subject by the arrival of the sent message:

> To have been informed is to be in a state of knowing something. Becoming informed denotes a change in what we know.
>
> (Buckland 107)

If "knowledge is intangible" (Buckland, 40), however, it is difficult to comprehend how such a change in "state" could be understood. This difficulty aside, we should note in regard to our discussion of systems in the next chapter that Buckland's definition of information follows the American pragmatist's notion of "understanding" as the overcoming of doubt and the having of an 'experience.' To be specific, it is John Dewey who often writes of understanding occurring through the overcoming of doubt and a change of state in the knower. "Becoming-informed" seems to denote an attitude shift along pragmatic lines. The possibilities for this change of state, however, say nothing about the "states" that are changing: what is the degree of that morphological change? What happens to the 'debris' state? The general conditions for this revolution or this metamorphosis of mental state ("change" is so general that it connotes either of these) cannot, I would argue, be accounted for with representational models of language and with 'transmission' models of communication.

Before concluding this chapter, I think that we should recognize how thoroughly some of the metaphysical and metaphorical conceptions we have been discussing penetrate classification theory. Perhaps one of the most extended studies of classification occurred within the work of the Classification Research Group (CRG) in the 1950s through the 1960s. Following Ranganathan, through the use of a faceted classification scheme such as PRECIS (Preserved Context Index System) classification was extended beyond the analytical confines of traditional genus-class relations and a term could now be multiply predicated, as well as predicate other terms, (thus making it very suitable for index searching also). Ranganathan's influence upon CRG was not just that of a distant influence. Ranganathan writes of "occasional visits and correspondence" with the group in his *Prolegomena* and the second issue of the CRG's *Bulletin* contains a paper, "Library Classification as a Discipline," given by Ranganathan at the International Study Conference on Classification for Information Retrieval during May 1957 at Dorking, Surrey, England, complete with a glossary for Ranganathan's writings, prepared by a Dr. Campbell. It is not my intention here to explore this link further than to note that questions raised in the first *Bulletin* are relative to the representational and organic assumptions of Ranganathan's colon classification and to the epistemic assumptions of classification as a whole. Two points may be picked out of the first *Bulletin* as to the question of representation:

1. Are we agreed that the correct way to index a specific subject is to analyze it into its elementary "substantives" or "isolates" and to represent the subject by a composite of these elements linked together by "operators" or "conjunctions" expressing relation?

2. What are the main problems connected with the symbolic representation of subjects?

These quotes show some doubts in the members' minds as to the problem of representation, but they seem in the end to have been limited to the pragmatic problem of how to make representation work better within classification schemata. We, however, might want to ask two other questions about representation within classification, the first, a general question in regard to classification (and one which, by principle, cannot be answered 'in general'), and the second, specifically in regard to the CRG.

First, since representations play not only representational roles but regulative roles within classification schemata, what are the boundaries of any classification universe as indicated by its primary classes, whether those primary classes perform synthetic functions or are the results of analytical methods? Second, what influence did Ranganathan's metaphysics have upon the CRG? It would be presumptuous to assume none. In the collection *Classification and Information Control: Papers Representing the Work of the Classification Research Group During 1960-1968*, we find organic metaphors in Helen Tomlinson's paper, "Concepts within Politics" (where "formal," organic bodies of government are privileged as proper government) (*Classification*, 68-72) and in E. J. Coates paper, "CRG Proposals for a New General

Classification," where an "outline of the scheme of integrative levels" for classification begins at the level of "fundamental particles" and moves through "nuclei," "atoms," "molecules," "molecular assemblages (natural objects and artifacts)," "cells," "organisms," "human beings," and ends, of course, with "human societies" (*Classification*, 21). Perhaps no more telling presence of organicism—and the circle of *episteme* and *phusis* in classification—can be found in the collection than in Helen Tomlinson's paper, "Problems Arising From First GCS Papers":

> None of the GCS papers has been concerned primarily with biological entities as its subject matter, and therefore the sequence of biological entities has not been further amplified. However, this group of entities, possibly more than any other, *suggests a natural sequence* of integrative levels, *and therefore no insurmountable problem is at present in evidence.*
>
> (Emphases added; *Classification*, 74)

Such "evidence" suggests the failure of the group to fully explore the foundations of their undertaking.

The next chapter of this paper will attempt a more speculative discussion of some issues of representation involved in systems theory and information theory, as the latter will be understood as a part of the former. Just as classifications are constructed within representational metaphysics and according to organic metaphors, so I would argue, systems theory complicates the rather static nature of classification by assuming a metaphor of dynamic 'flow' which 'gathers up' (Hegel's *Aufhebunq*) formerly representational entities within the acceptable coding of a larger dynamic structure.

Chapter 2   Systems, Metaphor, and Time

When Michael Buckland asks about the nature of information in the quote that began this essay, not only is his question immediately wrapped within a classical hermeneutic circle, but it follows a very specific metaphysical path. As Heidegger warned, the question of 'what is x?' immediately presupposes "a call to the thing itself"—and as Kant demonstrated, this is an impossible call to answer.[16] Further, following Rodolphe Gasché, we may argue that a reply to this question, the question of definition, defines a thing by what it is not, "as" something else ('x is y'; 'x as y,' 'information as thing,' 'information as process,' etc.). This metaphoricity of a thing in its definition is what Gasché in his book *The Tain of the Mirror* calls "the essential metaphoricity of being." The re-presentational nature of a being as something else, however, is often forgotten, first in the claim that a thing simply is itself and nothing else (i.e., that it has auto-effective presence), and second, that the thing follows, not precedes, that which it is like. In other words, as Derrida has argued, the philosophy of presence depends for its framing on a condition that it denies, but which it then coopts or excludes and passes into forgetfulness.

The philosophy of systems, what Heidegger calls the "will to systems" (Schelling, section A), begins with the universal systems of 19th century German Idealism and culminates in a contemporary view of systems that stresses local 'open systems' (systems characterized by 'outside' inputs and adaptively morphological 'self-organization' (Machlup & Mansfield, 46; Langlois, 595 ff.)). Systems, whether 'top-down,' or 'bottom up' depend on organic metaphors not only for their essential structural division into parts and wholes (Machlup, 43, Langlois, 582 ff., Day, 621) but for their teleological "purposive" (Robertson and Belkin, 200; Buckland, 66), predictive, performative, or prescriptive dynamics.[17] All these "p" terms denote, within different discursive and academic fields, the teleological dynamics of systems, whether that teleology be understood within terms of a closed system or a more evolutionary one. As Buckland argues in terms of data within record systems, "records are descriptions of how something is supposed to be" (Buckland, 59). Based on the prescriptivity of this "ought," systems theory is particularly inviting to moral and other ethical and political discourses when applied in the private and public spheres. Systems, as constructed metaphors, follow "as if" analyses. Thus, in our study of how systems theory in its practice constructs political and "everyday life" (say through 'organizational management,' or information 'flows') we are never far away from moral inscriptions.[18]

The prescriptiveness of systems, too, guarantees their fundamental sameness, namely that their essential design repeats over space and time. Systems are thus metaphorical in their repetition and indeed, 'are,' only as they themselves repeat. There would be no such thing as a system if endurance wasn't one of its initial properties. As Robert Cooper writes, "the compulsion to repeat [Freud's *Wiederholen*] is a call to order" (410). The "repetition compulsion" of systems is thus both intrinsic to their growth and the maintenance of their boundaries and being, as well as is symptomatic of the very instability and undecidability which characterizes presence. Namely, that systems must continually enframe the other in terms of the representations appropriate to a system in order to claim self-presence. This aporia and forgetfulness of the otherness of itself marks the groundings of systems in repetition and metaphoricity.[19]

From a top-down perspective (within an organic model), according to Machlup, systems provide for the "organization" of complex data (46). From this perspective they are idealistic models for theorizing phenomenon within "an image, termed a model" (Machlup, 44). Robertson and Belkin verify this understanding from a cognitive perspective regarding 'information.' Information for these two writers is "structure," "reflection," and "image," the latter term denoting "the mental conception that we have of our environment and ourselves in it" (198). Robertson and Belkin's understanding of mental 'structures' or (organic) 'states' as *imago* follows the path of cognitive science, where, as Machlup points out, the term "representation" plays a key role, denoting a symbolic understanding of *episteme*, largely derived from the artificial languages of computer science (Machlup, 34). The cognitive model posits the correspondence between a thing (or phenomenological 'state') and understanding, resulting in truth (*veritas*) (see Heidegger, "On The Essence of Truth"). 'Foggy states,' such as moods, 'emotions,' and certain other 'mental states' (e.g., pain)[20] are denoted as minor states to such phenomenon within cognitive science and information theory because these sciences are based in a representational tradition that is 'photocentric' (e.g., '*imago*') and are thus guided by visual metaphors of understanding (e.g., 'see what I mean?', etc.). (Unlike Heidegger, who, reacting to the metaphysics of representation and "onto-photo-logy" (Borch-Jacobsen, 56; Gasché, "photology"), posited mood as fundamental within the phenomenology of human being as *Dasein* (see *Being and Time*).) Coming out of, but closing the distance of medieval allegory, correspondence (as in the conduit metaphor) denotes two worlds that are present and can come to agreement. Such an epistemology makes use of a naive realism that philosophically goes as far back as Plato, including for its sight metaphors (see, of course, Plato's "allegory of the cave"). Correspondence, the medieval *adaequatio* is, at best, a paradox because it requires, while simultaneously denying, a ground outside of the corresponding entities in order for correspondence to occur.

While Robertson and Belkin's argument that information systems construct or shift imagistic mental states rests on metaphysical and mentalistic grounds that were shaky long before cognitive science developed in the 1960s and 1970s, it does introduce a structural perspective to the problem of information that is important. This importance is due to several factors. First it allows us to speak about information in terms of a structural system. Furthermore, this relation of information to systems is made specific in ordinary language as we can speak of both systems and information "flows" (as well as "chains") and speak of their functions in terms of "use" and "processing" (implying that both systems and information are pragmatic, teleological structures). Second, structural analysis moves us away from a notion of information-as-thing and toward a social analysis of information. Only from a social analysis can we begin to speak meaningfully of 'information-as-thing' in terms of represented entities or commodities constructed and valued by one or many economic (that is, systemic) constructs of power.[21][22] If we look carefully, this notion of social formations for systems and for information is actually intrinsic to any correspondence model (such as the conduit metaphor), as there must be some actual grounds for the 'states' to be and to correspond, and these grounds must, in some manner, be allowed to carry certain values. Such social 'constructions,' however, can be spoken of in other ways than that of systems (for example, habits and language itself)

As Sandra Braman suggests in her article "Defining Information," from a social perspective the former parts of systems (within the vocabulary of information: "information-as-thing") and the dynamics (information as force, information as "perception of a pattern," "information as process," etc.) are functions of power rather than units or moments in ideal systems.[23] As Braman argues, the construction of information systems is based on "excluding specific types of information, actors and actions at individual or several stages of the chain" (Braman, 237). This is true, but I would also add that the very will-to-system itself is symptomatic of power relations. As Churchman points out, systems axiomatically argue those values which are positively defined within them (563). Thus, the 'will-to-system' within the ideological construct of a systemic society would privilege the repetition and continuation of systemic values. Those claims lacking in systemic values would be automatically excluded from the system as neither positive nor negative values. (It is important to remember that systems must have negative values as well as positive ones, otherwise 'positive' makes no sense).

As Derrida argues in *Given Time: I. Counterfeit Money*, there is the acute problem of "what gives" (from Heidegger, "*es gibt*") in the 'given' of any systemic structure or economy. "What gives"—or rather as it often expressed by the violence of the economy, 'who gives,' in social economies—is that which is excluded and by exclusion defined simultaneously as both a 'who' and a 'what' (i.e., 'one of those').[24] Such exclusion both defines the meanings (i.e., choices) from which meaning will be produced within a system by selection, as well as marks the boundaries of that which can be said to be presently meaningful, as well as in the future, within a system and as a system. This is true of open systems as well as closed systems, save that in open systems there is a premium put upon normalizing the values of inputs according to the representational code(s) recognized by the system.

The very construction of systems by what they are not, however, leads to the notion of trace which Derrida has clearly articulated throughout his works. In our context, trace names the construction of that which has meaning or being (Greek, *ousia*), not out of auto-effective self-presence, but out of that which remains unnamable within, or as, the system. In Derrida's words, *différance* (deferral and difference—in both a temporal and spatial sense—) allows beings to 'be' in a positive manner of presence, and thus to have a certain temporality and identity in space (i.e., to have or take place). *Différance* is thus intrinsic to the notion of presence, or in Gasché's phrase, there is an essential metaphoricity to definition and presence that allows beings to 'be' in the sense (and within the prescriptive 'way') of presence.

This Being as essence through which beings come to be understood quantitatively and qualitatively (as we have seen with classification) is bound to the presupposition of a totality. Indeed, it is by this metaphysics that organisms are understood as autonomous wholes with parts and that organicism itself is privileged as a method in both classification and systems theory. We have seen in classification a rather static concept of such a metaphysics, and we have seen such an *episteme* peak in bibliography during the early 20th century. Indeed, as Schrader argues, the privilege of bibliography begins to drop in the post-War period, especially in the U.S., and gives way to the age of documents and then to information (Schrader, 231, table 1). This shift in vocabulary seems to indicate both the end of the 'metaphysics of the book' (books=knowledge=universe, an *episteme* which we can still see traces of in Ranganathan), as well as the breaking-up of what Lyotard in *The Postmodern Condition* calls (universal) "metanarratives" of knowledge.

As I have suggested throughout this paper, however, it would be historically incorrect to see the shift from the macro-management to the micromanagement of nature and mind as revolutionary. As Robins and Webster have argued, much of the positivist hype about the 'information age' involves assumptions of revolution. As I have argued, however, much of the metaphysical and metaphorical baggage of traditional subjectivity is carried over from classification into systems and information theory: organicism, correspondence theories of truth (and their conduit metaphors), representational theories of language, system autonomy, teleology; in sum, the philosophy of presence.

Robins and Webster argue the shift of subjective control from a single centralized agency (the appendixes of this paper hold several examples of bibliographic knowledge portrayed as the sun and its rays) to decentralized agencies as a shift from centralized management to decentralized management. For Robins and Webster, the information age carries with it not only arguments of self-empowerment, but also of an extended, and radically empowered form of scientific management, that is, a more powerful Taylorism (49 ff.). They further argue that decentralized control appropriates the individuals placed within a system much more completely than a centralized agency. As they point out, contemporary information systems promise to connect the larger capitalist marketplace to the individual, right into their home, thus further disrupting the former bourgeois division between public and private life. This deterritorialization of the individual in private, vis-à-vis the home, was of course predated by other electronic and telecommunication materials, such as radio, television, and most of all the telephone.[25] As Avital Ronell argues, such devices are uncanny (Heidegger and Freud, *"Unheimlich"*—literally, 'unhome-like'), as they allow one to not be at home even while being at home ("Learning," 71). Though, according to psychoanalysis, such 'invasions' always already take place in the social construction of the ego (*das Ich*) through language, the construction of personal being by production economics and mass consumer culture is accomplished in capitalist modernism and postmodernism by the reification of representation and the construction of time as presence. The home, which in bourgeois culture from the 18th and 19th century came to symbolize a sanctuary, even a virgin purity for being, thought, and ethics, away from the typing of personal identity by characteristics of systemic production, is now poised to become further 'on-line' with a commodities constructed marketplace through computerized information networks. As Robins and Webster point out, the becoming on-line of the former private sphere represents a further extension of capital into the private sphere of personal being and symbolizes the market's further control of the former public sphere. The ego will thus be constituted, more and more, and deeper and deeper, by for-profit commodity relations, rather than by nonrepresentational relationships with other human beings. The effects that such commoditization has upon ethics—which depend upon group feelings for individual responsibility, for example, have not really been thought through in anything but a superficial manner. Such appropriations erode what Robins and Webster term "social skills, knowledge, and self-sufficiency" (66), some of whose qualities do not depend on, and in fact are quite antithetical to, the representational and temporal characteristics of the market economy and systems in general.

Today, the blurring of 'information' and 'knowledge' seems symptomatic of this erosion. Contrary to two workers in information and retrieval—Buckland (41 ff.) and Meadow (23)—Machlup, for example, does not regard knowledge as a state of "certainty" or "belief" (a claim which echoes the philosophical tradition of subjectivity and representation), but rather, regards knowledge as (what Heidegger would call) a 'way' of thinking. This claim not only allies Machlup with early 20th century continental philosophers (such as Heidegger) and away from the claims of both 19th century positivism and idealism, but it allows the possibility of speaking about information and knowledge as distinct, though linked, ways through which meaning can occur. Machlup's argument is quite interesting (643 ff.) and should be read in full, but I think it can be summed up by two quotes. First, Machlup writes, "information is acquired by being told, whereas knowledge can be acquired by thinking" (644). Second, "Any kind of experience—accidental impression, observations, and even 'inner experience' not induced by stimuli received from the environment—may initiate cognitive processes leading to changes in a person's knowledge. Thus, knowledge can be acquired without new information being received" (644). Machlup's phonocentric inscription of information ("being told") certainly cannot be exempted from modernism's experience with the telephone, but it is the larger context of information's definition within modernism and postmodernism, from Shannon's mathematical definition of "information" while at Bell Labs to information's metaphorical transfers to contexts of interpersonal and social communication, that we are concerned. Within these two statements, Machlup defines information, distinct from knowledge, by the concept of a line of meaning through which one is told and can tell again (in much the same way that persons or computers can be linked together on a network, or that shop workers were linked together within Taylor's scientific management, towards the goal of standardizing labor so as to standardize, i.e. repeat, the product). Here, language is constructed for a consistent system of users (be they person or machine), rather than as an interpretative medium whose function is to generate, rather than retrieve meaning. In much the same way, the complexities of classical rhetoric have been largely expelled from organizational communication and replaced by 'bullet' forms of rhetoric which are supposed to represent clear and distinct atomic units of meaning, mimicking the artificial languages of the technical sciences. Language within information systems plays the exclusive roles which Braman attributes to it: homogenization and *linkage* of both producers and users within a system of meaning; *processing* of new data by selecting, transforming, and selecting again the data according to the representational form appropriate to the system (i.e., in-forming data); maintaining the *'flow'* of informed data, and thus minimalizing the autonomy, resistance, and interpretative agencies of the persons or machines within the system; and promoting the value of a pragmatic *'use'* over all other values within the system and 'outside' the system.

Not surprisingly, each of the above values for language within a system preserves the integrity and supposed autonomy of the system at hand and of systemics in general. As we have seen, however, systems, as any form of presence, depend on what they are not for what they proclaim they are. They are, as Robert Cooper puts it, wholes defined by holes, presences defined by internal differences rather than selfpresence and auto-affection (402). The privilege that certain forms of language have today is a result of the forgetting of the grounds for systems and the narrowing of language to that of systemic or pseudo-systemic language.[26] If, as Heidegger argued, "language is the house of Being," then the language of information, of 'clear' and 'simple' presentation, is first of all the being of radical presence and self-representation within social systems. The inherent resistance of language to semantic totality at levels of vocabulary or syntax is denied in a systems approach, even though meaning within a system is logically dependent on that which it excludes as 'nonmeaningful' for its economic functioning and rights.

After the initial selection of the system itself, there are two main 'internal' components of systems. The first component is the transformation of individuals made up of schisms of differences—whether they be data or persons, 'creators' or 'users'—to representational values for the system. Cooper, I think rightly, relates such 'objectification' to 'homogenization' and abjection in individual humans; a certain 'mean-ness' given to personal identity through typology (412). It is the preparation of a being toward recognizability by a system, according to a "way of seeing" (413). The second component is the notion of force, dynamics, or desire within systems. This second component is synonymous with the concept of time in systems, namely, time as a stream of presences or 'nows.' The 'now' in systems has both a temporal and a spatial sense of presence, because the now is ultimately constituted by the represented data or persons at any 'moment of time.' Representational being and the 'now' are synonymous within systems. Thus, the flow, history, or time of systems can be analyzed into infinitely divisible parts.

The transformation of individuals within systems involves their being reconstructed as a representational or 'in-formational' value which the system will recognize. In social production mechanisms, this transformation is encouraged by the leveling of distinctions between persons and materials within a production mechanism.[27] Non-systemic temporal values, for example, must be converted into representations that function as present 'nows' within the serial temporality of systems. As Robins and Webster argue, it is the temporality of the clock which came to value the labor and social being of workers within capital (50). As they argue, the "capitalist annexation of time and space" since the industrial revolution has divided work time from leisure time. More importantly, however, this annexation has reinforced a sense of temporality based on the 'now' of productive presence.

The temporality of presence is very usable for mechanical and electrical devices which run by a binary logic, but it has been argued, at least by Heidegger and Freud, that this sense of time is not fundamental to a human sense of 'the present' which has the form of a non-quantitative compromise between memories and intents, traditions and non-contingencies.[28] Critical modernism opposed itself to the reification of the temporality of presence by production economies, and as Lyotard suggests in the preface to his collection *The Inhuman*, nothing less than the meaning of the 'human' is once again at stake in the "metaphysics of development" (7) and the meaning of the concept of 'information.' This is why I believe Derrida writes in his proposal for the International College of Philosophy that "telecommunications" be investigated for its relation to the techne of Western metaphysics, namely destiny, destination, trans-mission, and *Geist* ("Sendoffs," 32 ff). (*Geist* can be is translated as "Mind" or "Spirit"; for Hegel, in *The Phenomenology of Spirit*, *Geist* is both interpersonal desire and the universal force of history, as these two levels are reflective of one another within the philosophical system of the sciences.)

In his lecture *The Concept of Time*, given at the Marburg Theological Society in 1924, Heidegger foreshadowed many of the themes of *Being and Time* (1927). Foremost, is Heidegger's concern with human temporality and its relation to the quantitative construction of time as a series of 'nows,' symbolized by the clock. For Heidegger, a reign of the temporality of presence moves human beings (as *Dasein* (existence)) away from a more fundamental experience of time. For Heidegger, the transformation of time away from a fundamental human experience toward a universal quantitative measure is shown by our asking '*what* is time?' instead of 'how is time' for someone, or even, 'who is time?' (*The Concept of Time*, 22E). With the quantitative measure of time, death too is removed from human being, because, for Heidegger, it is the anxiety toward death which throws us back on our finitude and gives us *Dasein's* authentic experience of time. As an experience of finitude, time is specific for each human existence, each *Dasein*. For Heidegger, the privileging of clock time in Western metaphysics and technology leads to forgetting the more fundamental experience of time upon which this quantitative sense of time is founded.

In Hegel's system, for example, time is wholly made up of the 'now.' The whole of the system is the serial totality of 'nows' and the parts of the system are the division of the totality into its atomic temporal units ('now'). The notion of 'now' is easily transferred along gradients of measure within an organic universe, as the 'now' can signify the temporal presence of a second, a minute, an hour, a day, a lifetime, an era, or even time itself. What is important is that the increment of the 'now' be understood as an organic unit of size, as a part or even the whole of a totality, rather than as an index for scale.[29] This metaphysics of time descends from the Aristotelian paradox of time where "now" signifies both the presence of 'time itself' and the presence of atomic units of time. Furthermore, as Derrida fleshes out from Aristotle, Hegel, and foremost Heidegger, for this tradition of time the present as 'now' carries with it a strong sense of being as a present substance (*ousia*), a culmination of all that was and a predictive of all that is to come (Derrida, "Ousia and Gramme: Notes on a Note from *Being and Time*"). Each present carries with it a presence that is self-sufficient and complete, despite the paradox of time and the entirety of the 'system of time.'

For Heidegger, there are social implications for *Dasein* defined according to the temporality of presence. Heidegger calls the quantification of time in public space the 'everyday' (*Alltäglichkeit*) or vulgar notion of time, which is a time of hustle and bustle, from one moment ('now') to the next, according to the clock. For Heidegger, this represents a homogenizing of time, and thus, a homogenizing of human specificity:

> No one is himself in everydayness. What someone is, and how he is, is nobody: no one and yet everyone with one another. Everyone is not himself. This Nobody by whom we ourselves are lived in *everydayness* is the 'One' (*das 'Man'*). One says, one listens, one is in favor of something, one is concerned with something.

(*The Concept of Time*, 9E)

And yet, Heidegger argues, this giving over to the other leaves one unsatisfied:

> I never have the Dasein of the other in the original way, in the sole appropriate way of having which Dasein has: I never *am* the other.

(*The Concept of Time*, 11 E, trans. modified)

In *The Concept of Time*, the quantitative notion of time is marked by two characteristics. The first characteristic is the "irreversibility" of time. Temporal series, represented by metaphors of lines or 'flows' (as in systems) are irreversible, and their temporality is understood as highly predictive and determinate. This historicism leads, for Heidegger, to us not only seeing ourselves 'in time,' but also to the devaluation of time as an agency for 'self-authenticity.' Time no longer is bound to Being, and individual human existences are no longer thrown back upon their individual specificities by the experience of time in death. Second, the quantification of time homogenizes *Dasein* as one now among many nows, one presence among many presences which stretch endlessly into the past and trail endlessly into the future. Thus, time loses any sense of measure because it is understood as measure itself. (The metaphor of the time 'line' becomes useful here.) No time has any other value than any other time, no times lead to the construction or reevaluation of other times; historicity ceases to have meaning. Indeed, temporal senses of earlier and later begin to fade into quantitative measures of before and after:

> In the arithmetic sequence, for example, the 3 is before the 4, the 8 after the 7. Yet the 3 is not earlier than 4 on this account.... Once time has been defined as clock time then there is no hope of ever arriving at its original meaning, again.
>
> (18E-19E).

This wrestling of the notion of time away from an individual existence (*Dasein*) represents the "cast[ing] of time into the bad present (*Gegenwart*) of the everyday" (14E).

Understanding this construction of time based on the metaphysical conceptions of the 'now' (as presence) is important because it lays the groundwork for understanding the temporality of systems, their representational construction of data and persons within, and their privilege in contemporary culture. As we have argued, systems are prescriptive and need 'positive' data—that is, what they 'recognize' as 'clear and distinct' data—in order to process material and to 'flow' as a system. As we have seen, however, system values gain their privilege—and come to constitute a system—only by selecting and repressing other values. As Derrida argued, the giving of time—or time as a given, as a presence, as something we 'live in'—is possible only as time is a trace of a more original difference.[30] As Hegel and German Idealism recognized, systems not only represent themselves as auto-effectively present, but within their organic structures they claim to be constituted by presence itself—as 'parts' and as 'whole.'

Only by understanding the temporality of representation in systems, and as systems, can we begin to see systems as the temporalization of classification schemata according to the 'now.' But also, only by understanding the temporality of systems in terms of representation can we begin to understand their cybernetic relation to human beings. Systems are not merely tools of human beings nor random intellectual configurations of 'our time' nor even objective 'states' of 'nature,' but instead, are constructions of human relations, power, and metaphysics. It is important to understand the construction of time by systems, for as Foucault noted, "Power is articulated directly into time; it assures control and guarantees its use" (cited in Robins and Webster, 50). The historical relation between various historical *epistemes* and time has yet to be explored, and the study of the relation of systems technology and of information to time is still fairly recent.

Intrinsic to Hegel's conception of a system in *The Phenomenology of Geist* is historical force and intersubjective desire. Desire is, for Hegel, both a particular manifestation of historical force and an attribute that makes up the system's totality. It is not my intention here to analyze desire within Hegel's system, though I think such a study would shed light on the nature of force in systems. Nor is it my intention here to open up the problem of the psychoanalysis of information, although I think that such a study would bear results not only for systems theory but for psychoanalysis. (After all, psychoanalysis was born out of theories of electro-neural biology,[31] and its vocabulary is that of circuitry: libidinal flows, resistance to the psychoanalytic/social cure, paralysis in parts of the social body (i.e., individual bodies), etc...)[32] But it wouldn't be enough to offer a narrative of the construction of persons through systemic time, however, if we couldn't also account for the need of that time in individual human beings. And the concept of 'desire,' understood as a force operative to systems, I think, illuminates how it is that human beings are cyborgs with the systemic tools that they produce and use. After all, even as Heidegger was aware, the hustle and bustle of serial time is not totally other to human beings, though its omnipresence can be alienating. Whether this mode of temporality is the most fundamental sense of temporality for human beings or not, the clock is still deeply familiar to human beings. The clock, as all tools, is not simply an object, but is cybernetically part of human being. The hustle and bustle which clock time represents can be addicting, like any drug, only because it addresses a need.

The 'now' which makes up clock time is, in its particularity and as a general system, binary and thus, exclusive. In fact, we could argue, that this binary logic is itself possible only because data (or the particular 'now') is understood as a presence that must yet be 'caught up in the flow.' In Buckland's words, represented data ('information') must be both "information-as-thing" and "information-as-process."

Delay and ambivalence within systems is understood as a negative attribute. But if representations within systems are to simultaneously be both states and within the flow of a process, then delay and ambivalence are ontological necessities for them. The delay caused by the autonomy of materials must be slight, but this slight delay is in fact necessary for the continual 'flow' of a system (and of its time). Consider, for instance, first, if a system had no new inputs, and second, if a system had no recognizable parts. In the first case, that of a closed system, energy or time would quickly cease to exist within a system, and consequently the system itself would cease to exist. In the second case, according to the organic metaphor of systems we would cease to have a system without parts. Thus, there must be *some* autonomy and resistance vis-à-vis new inputs and parts in order for a system to flow and to be.

From the viewpoint of an individual person, the flow of time presents a structure very similar to subjective desire, at least as desire has been conceived as a drive (Freud, *Trieb*) or a force. Desire can only be when it can be projected onto an object or state. Say for example, you desire a car. Once you have the car, you no longer desire it. Desire, as noted by Freud, Lacan, and even Hegel, requires—to a certain degree— its own repression, its own being-controlled, for it to be. I would propose that social systems not only fulfill this condition of repression, always keeping the object just slightly out of reach from the subject in time, but also fulfill the other condition of both systems and desire, namely, to have a limited number of entities, *qua* 'objects,' for desire.

Whether desire forms systems or systems form desire is a difficult question, leading to a circle of responses, a trace of metaphors. Both notions are formed by representation and a representational sense of temporality. Both notions evolve at the beginning of the 19th century and both triumph in Western cultures in the 20th century. Both notions claim presence and suppress their metaphoricity, and even as they themselves form a hermeneutic circle, that structure itself, as a structure, repeats classification, which repeats Aristotelian definition, which repeats... what? The search for an origin is futile because the trace is itself that of the forgotten origin.

In brief, I would argue that the structure of delayed but ultimate satisfaction which systems provide is an addictive structure for human beings acting within the mode of desire. Such a promise of satisfaction is only possible by an always already selected set of possibilities within an always already possible future. Desire requires objects, a future, and a delay in order to flow and to be. Systems require objects, a future, and a delay in order to flow and to be. From a viewpoint of temporality and representation, desire and systems have an identical ontological structure. This shared ontology allows individuals to 'enter into' system and to 'ride' with them in their 'drive' (*Trieb*).

The cybernetic relationship between personal psychology in the mode of desire and social or mechanical systems is neither an abomination of 'human nature' nor a mere accident of technological invention. The addictive drives which narrative realist literature, computers, and bureaucratic organizations have for human beings are legendary and cannot be denied, even if we are aware that other modes of being for human being are possible and are necessary (see Avital Ronell's *Crack Wars*). The 'invasion' of the market system into the home via information technology, which Robins and Webster deplore, cannot simply be explained by the capitalist construction of human beings into consumers and into commodities, because that repression would also then require explanation as to its success. As Ronell argues, what the television makes explicit is that we were never always at home alone with ourselves anyway (Ronell, "Learning...", 71), and even when we thought we were (as in Heidegger, the encounter with death), we then went the 'other way.' This 'other way,' guarantees a home—even if in its own uncanniness (*unheimlichkeit*) such a program is utopian, fictive, or simply regulative for desire. This guarantee of futurity in an object is what systems (as well as realist narratives) promise through their temporal structures. The addictive quality which that promise then poses for our desire—which, by its very structure, ambivalently wants to be home and not be at home at the same time—is something that has to be thought about carefully and negotiated within the *episteme* of systems and information. As Lyotard argues, we are always located within "nodal points" of multiple narrative structures and systems (*The Postmodern Condition*, 15). But, I think, it would be shortsighted not to understand that such nodal points owe their 'point' status to 'resistances' or 'reserves' that are not points. The nodal points which humans form within systems are only possible because there are reserves 'beyond' representation which allow representations to be.

Utilizing Heidegger's critique of traditional metaphysics and science's mode of revealing, Cooper writes:

> Such revealing is aimed at the securing of certainty through the making secure of a constant reserve. Further, this process tends towards finality through the construction of large-scale systems of certainty which seek to master what remains of uncertainty: a continuous chain of terms is forged which must reinforce each term's certainty.
>
> (Cooper, 414)

As Derrida reminds us, we are really neither 'within' economic/systemic structures nor 'outside' of them. Such structures are not only historical projections of epistemes upon nature but, in turn, constitute functional social forms for the being of *episteme* and psychology itself. Ontologically speaking, however, the presence of systemic structures marks a difference which logically comes before them, and by which they can be bounded. In the 'will-to-system,' like the visions of classification, we are caught within a hermeneutic circle of *episteme* and nature. Such a circle itself marks by its very presence a site where it is not. Extrication from the circle, if not from the being of systems, is a possible historical move.

Conclusion

This paper has attempted to raise questions concerning the relation of metaphor and metaphysics to classification schemata and information systems within the Western tradition, especially since the late 18th century.

However, two questions remain. First, why did the shift from classification to systems theory, which occurred in the biological sciences as early as the beginning of the 19th century, take so long to occur in bibliography? And second, what were the conditions for the collapse of "metanarratives" (Lyotard) of classification in bibliography and the rise of micronarratives governed by systems theory? These are very wide-ranging questions, and I will only speculate as to their answers.

Speaking from a postmodern critique of subjectivity (and thus, a tradition of Romanticism and modernism), such a critique would be expected to begin furthest away from subjectivity. In other words, a critique of the hermeneutic circle of *episteme* and nature will always begin with nature. The reason for this is the problem of critiquing method by method. In subjectivity method is located with (though not identical to) the subject. Thus, only with the critique of the subject proper could method even be approached as a problem, and consequently, knowledge come into crisis.

Bibliographically, the privilege of the book for centralized authority has religious roots at least as far back as the Hebraic and Christian traditions. As we see with S. R. Ranganathan, knowledge was represented singularly by groups of books, and as a totality by libraries and classification schemata. The displacement of knowledge from books to vocabularies, as occurred in the move from classification schemata to indexes, represents both an epistemological collapse of belief in subject and author centered metanarratives, as well as the success of scientific management and document and information retrieval technology, especially following the Second World War.

The shift from macro-narratives to micronarratives presents methodological problems of scale. I have attempted to argue that the general conditions of systems theory, and subsequently, information theory, do not fully acknowledge this methodological problem, and instead, rely on representational models to constitute values for both the morphology and the functionality of systems and knowledge. Moreover, I have attempted to argue that such a shift from macro to micronarratives is not as radical as it might seem, and instead is still rooted in concepts of representation and organicism which traditionally constitute the Western metaphysical and scientific enterprise.

But I would also like to argue that there is a seductive call to this scientific "enframing" (Heidegger) of human beings themselves, and that contrary to humanism, 'freedom' is often experienced by human beings as being-reified and being-controlled. ("Seduction" suggests that science's denial of its frame is itself wished for.) As I have tried to argue, systems offer to human beings two conditions for augmenting their desire: 1) the narrowing and selection of objects for desire, and 2) the pragmatic probability of fulfilling that desire in an 'objective' serial temporality. I have argued that both these conditions are axiomatic to our traditional notion of time, especially as it has been experienced since the 19th century. This congruence of temporal 'flows' between systems and desire is, however, historically specific, and it is unclear if we can argue desire as a metaphor for systems or systems as a metaphor for desire. It is clear from our experience, however, especially with the enframing of word processors and computers, that systems, like earlier narrative structures are seductive and addictive and that they answer a call or a need within human beings for feeling in control-toward-an-object while that experience itself is enframed.

Though it is true that micronarratives can provide objects of desire at highly individual levels, I would agree with Robins and Webster that we must examine both the historical and the ontological relations between macro-narratives and micronarratives in order to understand the relation between systems theory and desire.

This paper has attempted to epistemologically investigate this relation at the historical shift between classification and systems, and knowledge and information, especially in regard to bibliography. I have argued that a study of this shift is not enough, and that it is necessary to understand the ontological structures common to the two parts of this 'shift' in order to understand that this shift is not a 'revolution' but a continuity. Thus, the problems of structure, representation, and time have been central in this paper. Lastly, influenced by Derridean poststructuralism, I have tried to speak of this continuity even while acknowledging the position of this paper at the critical margins of it.

In sum, this paper has tried to address fundamental issues within information science that, I feel, have not been satisfactorily addressed in the past, and in fact, have been prematurely closed. In this way, its intent was to open the problem of the philosophy of information on this subject, so that information policy can be developed in other than an historical and philosophical vacuum.

Endnotes

1. The double reflection of the hermeneutic circle not only occurs in classification, of course, but also in systems. As Robert Cooper writes,

    > In systems thinking, a presupposition of systemness organises the world in its own image and this has important consequences for how we define information. (496)

2. See Donna Haraway, "A Manifesto for Cyborgs" and "Overhauling the Meaning Machines: An Interview with Donna Haraway" for a critical discussion of human cyborgs.

    The humanist position in regard to technology is so well known as to need no citation. As to the understanding of technology as 'tool,' see for example Buckland, "Each tool, each technology..." (70). Buckland is not unique here, and I cite this example because the understanding of technology as a mere tool *qua* thing will become part of a more general methodology toward the question of technology and information which Buckland engages in (i.e., the question of 'what is x?').

    Our position here attempts a third, critical position, which understands humanism and technology as part of the same metaphysics. For a defense of this position see Jean-Francois Lyotard's introduction to *The Inhuman*.

3. For historical charts showing schemata of knowledge and bibliographic classification in the West, see Sayers, *Manual of Classification*. It is interesting to note that whereas Sayers understands Bacon's classification schema of history, poetics, and philosophy (from the faculties of memory, imagination, and reason) as "a history of the record of thought as it was at the date of its appearance in 1605 (Sayers, 129), Ranganathan, from a somewhat non-European tradition simply says that "it is not socio-centered.... It is psychology centered" (*Prolegomena*, 394).

4. In the fifth chapter of his *Manual of Classification*, Sayers writes,

    > We believe that the Universe as it came from the Creative Mind was not a chaos; but an orderly system of things. [Sayers gives the Genesis account of the division of light from darkness.] From this example we draw our first definition of classification... We know, indeed, that Nature has her groups of things, planets which move by the same laws, plants which have the same characteristics, animals which have a definite and invariable structure; and this grouping of like things is the classifying process of whatever Creative Power we may believe to be at the source of the universe. (Sayers 63)

    It is interesting to note the Aristotelian and medieval doctrine of final cause for nature that Sayers presupposes; a doctrine argued against by Spinoza in the 17th century (*Ethics*, Part I), yet resurrected in the late 18th century with the notion of order in the universe and turned into epistemology during the late 19th and early 20th century's scientific positivism.

Also of interest is Sayers' statement that animals have "definite and invariable structure." Though this seems to be an argument against evolution, evolution is a very important concept for Sayers (Sayers, 48 ff.). Evolution provides Sayers with evidence of "homology," a term which denotes common class characteristics (proceeding back to the beginning of creation: "The creator in his primal works created a few simple forms, and from these have generated less simple forms...." (Sayers, 48)).

5. The positivist ramifications of this metaphysics are, of course, clear, i.e., the desire and real possibility of human beings to have a complete knowledge of "all there is" (including method itself (e.g., within a universe of order, knowledge classification)) and therefore, by definition, for humans to be God.

Heidegger terms this drive the "onto-theological" basis of Western metaphysics and science. For Freud, this ambivalent pleasure/death drive (*Trieb*) is a repetition of an infantile desire to return to the pre-Oedipal, and even pre-breast, state.

I think Heidegger is quite right in locating a supreme example of the tradition of 'thought thinking thought' in Hegel's system of the philosophical sciences, especially in the notion of Absolute Knowledge which is exactly this thinking of thought's method by thought (see Hegel's *Phenomenology of Spirit*).

6. Sayer's emphasis and repetition of this phrase is, of course, symptomatic of both the fragility of this notion as well as the ideological and political forces which are needed—and the violence which is called upon in grammar and in 'knowledge'—to enforce and perpetuate it. We will later see in this chapter the critical role classification plays in upholding various metaphysical, political, and theological discourses in the West. Sayers writes, for example,

> We have now to consider the bearing of all we have studied up to the present upon library classification. Again and again we have emphasized the fact that the material of classification is the whole of knowledge—that is, the material of knowledge classification. We may now say that a classification of books is a knowledge classification with adjustments made necessary by the physical form of books.
>
> (Sayers, 72)

7. In regard to the metaphor of the chain of being, Lovejoy writes:

> It was in the eighteenth century that the conception of the universe as a 'Chain of Being,' and the principles which underlay this conception—plenitude, continuity, gradation, attained their widest diffusion and acceptance.
>
> (Lovejoy 183)

8. For metaphor within biological evolution theory and cladistics, see Robert J. O'Hara, "Telling the Tree: Narrative Representation and the Study of Evolutionary History" and "Representations of the Natural System in the Nineteenth Century."

9. This "problem" of scale will reoccur in our discussions of systems in regard to communication models based on metaphor, repetition, and re-presentation (such as the conduit metaphor). To be specific, it will occur in regard to the 'giving' of language vis-à-vis systems, and conversely, the privileging of systems that 'give' language as an economy of exchange (i.e., language as 'in-formation'). Derrida notes this problem of the gift in regard to language in *Given Time: I. Counterfeit Money*:

> For example, one might wonder if the same semantic order governs the logic of the gift whether it is under the regime of to have or to be. In general, it is thought that one can give only what one has, what one possesses as one's own, and give it to the other who, in his or her turn, can thus have it, come into possession. The very paradox of 'giving what one does not have' which we have already talked about, has the value of paradox only because of what links, in common sense, giving with having. One might wonder if the same semantic order governs locutions that, on the contrary, imply the transfer of what one is to the other who takes—or becomes what is thereby given to him or her. Think of the expression 'to give oneself' of the metonymies or synecdoches concerning partial 'objects,' the fragments or signs of what one is and which one can give as something one has, abandons, or lets be taken. All the figures of this tropic are difficult to contain within the limits of a rhetoric the margins or 'terms' of which can no longer, in principle and in all rigor, be fixed.

(*Given Time*, 48-49)

10. Spinoza's criticism of infinite substance can be found in Part I of his *Ethics*.

11. See Michael J. Reddy, "The Conduit Metaphor—A Case of Frame Conflict in Our Language About Language."

12. For the primary text in structural linguistics, see of course, Ferdinand de Saussure's *Course in General Linguistics*. Derrida's famous critique of the remanent symbolism in Saussure, especially in regard to Saussure's conception of speech as the articulation of thought occurs, among other places, in *Of Grammatology*. In a slightly different context, Ludwig Wittgenstein critiques symbolist/representational theories of language (his starting point is St. Augustine's picture theory of language) by the notion of "language games" in *Philosophical Investigations*. "Language games," however, can themselves become nominalized; see for example Jean-Francois Lyotard's *The Postmodern Condition*, where "language games" is virtually synonymous with "systemics."

13. For an analysis of the sacrificial nature of representation, especially in regard to 'animals,' see Jean-Luc Nancy's interview with Jacques Derrida, "Eating Well." Georges Bataille's writings, of course, explore this theme, as well as sections of Nietzsche's writings (especially in his professions of extreme nausea in regard to the Western metaphysical tradition of representation).

14. We may note that the term "retrieval" is important here. We speak of retrieval as the bringing of a tangible 'thing' back to a spot from which the object was originally cast. Within this metaphor, both the "object" nature (Buckland's "information-as-thing") of knowledge or information, as well as the reconstituted object of the retrieval, are signified. Needless to add, the non-human connotations of the notion of 'retriever' (as canine or as machine) may want to be explored as information professionals come to define themselves and be defined within the role of information retrievers. One may want to ask, for example how the game of 'fetch' is being carried out, or, how 'the human' is being understood within a cybernetic 'game' of information production.

15. For Ranganathan, classification builders are "geniuses." Ranganathan's term harkens back to Plato's philosopher-king: the knower of knowledge who is able to assign each their own most proper function (or subject area) within the *polis*, except of course, Ranganathan's philosopher-king's 'city' is that of "the universe of knowledge"—both actual and potential. This may seem quite presumptuous, after all, wasn't Ranganathan one of these very people? But it is here that Ranganathan's thought becomes very mystical (not that the 18th century category, "genius," isn't already—after all, genius is, according to Kant, "nature's darling" (*Critique of Judgment*, section 318)). "Genius" for Ranganathan (again, echoing Kant in his third critique) comprehends the manifold of phenomenon, both at once in its sublime infinity and in its parts, and is able to embody this experience in finite forms of order appropriate to the taste of 'his' time. Ranganathan seems to describe the same 'ability' in both Indian and Western traditions, in the first quote even having a missing link between the two "types" of human being:

> Humanity has at intervals thrown forth supermen—Indian tradition calls them *Rhishis*; Frank Townsend uses the word *Urthmen* to denote a transitory type between solely intellectual men and the *Rishis*—with a mental feature—or is it supramental?—different from the primary senses and the intellect and capable of taking in infinite dimensions directly and unmediated by the limiting concepts developed by the infinite…. The term mystic experience…appears to be the only English one.
>
> (*Philosophy*, 93)
>
> How to select just those relevant characteristics for the construction of the associated scheme of characteristics that is likely to give us the most helpful scheme of classification. There can be no

> definite answer to this question, as obviously there can be no *a priori* rules for hitting upon the most helpful characteristics. Generally, it depends on genius; but, other things being equal, those with more knowledge and experience are more likely to have the flair to reject the less helpful characteristics.
>
> (*Prolegomena*, 55)

In Ranganathan's writing, the category of "genius" often plays the role of an example in explicating category definitions and intensional "chains." Despite the appeal to a logic of difference, another exclusionary "entity," "idiot," is usually chosen in order to define the representation of "genius." As in the Western tradition, "genius" is masculinely inscribed, though interestingly, in Ranganathan's order it is exclusionary of not only women, but non-adults, too. As with "idiot," the category "genius" defines itself by exclusion within an order of children, adolescents, and women. In fact, the following order of "entities" is remarkable for its illogic and prejudice if one understands the given classes as mutually exclusive:

> Let us imagine a well-guided stock-room. When the first kind of specialist enters, he wants the gangway guides to show the names of entities like Children, Adolescents, Women, Genius, Idiots, etc., so that he can walk into the gangway in which he is interested, say Genius.
>
> (*Philosophy*, 90)

16. On Heidegger's critique of method according to the form 'what is x?' see the beginning of "What is Metaphysics?" and the end of *The Concept of Time*. Also, Heidegger's critique of "the call 'to the thing itself'" in Hegel and Husserl's philosophies in "The End of Philosophy and the Task of Thinking," part II.

17. Two very important points should be made here. First, because system theories tend to assume the prescriptiveness of systemic structures, positive and normative values become blurred (Machlup, 35). This problem becomes acute when political and social 'policy,' for example, are understood solely in terms of systemics. (For an argument that stresses the non-organic being of communities and the non-teleological functions of politics, see Jean-Luc Nancy, *The Inoperative Community*.)

Second, as Churchman argues, the first axiom of systems is that systems define not only x, but all the results of x, such as y. This is because systems, especially engineering information systems (of which, Machlup and Mansfield argue, 'information theory,' in general, and 'communication' theory were incorrectly modeled off of (51 ff.)) arrive at positive values through selection and probability. It is important to remember, however, that such selection not only occurs through the process of a system, but occurs by the very construction of a system (i.e., certain values are repressed or excluded so that the processed variables within a system could even be). Needless to add, the construction of time in systems is thus highly causal and deterministic. It is on this axiom that 19th century philosophical systems, such as Hegel's, could make claims into the future—a unique but often overlooked aspect within the history of Western philosophy. Arguments of futurity also share this metaphysics of systems theory, and thus, are often self-fulfilling because of what they already assume as the possibility of truth. (On the socially repressive, politically conservative, and financially rewarding business of futurism, see Andrew Ross, "Getting the Future We Deserve," *Socialist Review* 91/1.)

18. For the work of poetics against "as if" structures, see my article, "'Against' Public Information: Barrett Watten's *Under Erasure*," in *Aerial's* (Washington, D.C.) critical anthology on Watten's work (forthcoming in spring 1993).

19. Robert Cooper's analysis of what he calls (after psychoanalysis) systems' "repetition compulsion" is quite remarkable and should certainty be quoted at length:

> Let us note that the compulsion to repeat is a call to order. The order in this case is the division that the subject must assume in order to know itself. Let us recall that Freud's term for the repetition compulsion is *Wiederholungszwang*. It is significant for us that *Wiederholung* (repetition) draws together several separate ideas: "again," "against," (*wieder, wider*) and collect (*holen*), thus identifying repetition and recollection. Now, *wieder* is also cognate with the English "wide" and "wider" and thus suggests the sense of expanding in order to contain more; the repetition here is not mere recurrence of the same but invokes the idea of "least effort" in which an undecidable "double" is objectified into the "singularity" of a wider frame. We can illustrate this operation through Rubin's profiles where the instability created by the oscillations of the shared faces is held in place by the wider frame of the page; without the support of the page's frame the observing subject would be lost in a vertigo of continuous vacillation. The act of recollection thus involves the subject in an act of division which entrails two steps: (1) the prior preparation of an object (only) through which the subject can later appear to itself—"a retroversion effect by which the subject becomes at each stage what he was before and announces himself—he will have been—only in the future perfect tense" (Lacan, *Ecrits* (English), 306, ["Subversion of the Subject and Dialectic of Desire"]); (2) the attenuation and simplification of the ambiguous and contradictory structure of difference, i.e., the finitizing a compulsive force (*Zwang*) and which operates automatically and without our conscious knowledge. Thus, order is peremptory. (410-411)

I would agree with Cooper's subjectification of systems, because of the teleological structures of systems, and with that, their reflectivity. Projection is an innate quality of systems due to selectivity. Projection does not only allow growth, but allows the 'objectification' of beings in terms of the representational qualities 'recognized' by the system.

More generally, Cooper's work is quite remarkable among the literature of information and systems theory, for it attempts to account for *différance* within the logic of systems. I would disagree with Cooper's understanding of Derridean "difference" (sic.) as dialectic (very strongly), with a certain eliding of psychoanalysis's economic (systems) characteristics, and with his Lacanian understanding of "information" as the filling in of an ontological lack or need (*manque*) based on language's own infinity and fundamental undecidability (404 ff.) (I feel this not only elides the question of knowledge too easily, but also elides the question of psychoanalysis's systematicity), but on the whole, his paper is remarkably good and highly recommended.

20. "Pain" provides a sticky problem for representational theories of thought and language. As we all know, pain is purely performative; when we are well it is difficult to remember pain. Pain is difficult to represent without creating its actual condition; it can't be spoken of "as" something else very meaningfully, though it can elicit sympathy through dramatic mimesis. George Miller, in a letter within Machlup and Mansfield's anthology, speaks about "symbolically represented cognition vs. primal, nonsymbolic represented cognition" (Miller, 59). How "representation" can be spoken of as "nonsymbolic" while preserving its almost exclusive symbolist connotations within cognitive science, I'm not sure. As philosopher and metapsychologist Rom Harré writes in his book *Personal Being*:

> The limitations of cognitive psychology arise from disparities between its source model, the general computation machine treated system-theoretically, and the client, a human being.... There seems to be no way that the necessary unities of human psychological functioning, the foundations of personal being, can be expressed in the concepts available within this framework.
>
> (Harré, 15)

As Machlup and Mansfield argue, cognitive science's dependence on computer simulation has created many difficulties in erecting models of intention and emotion. This difficulty may not be preventable. The concept of "mental states" has to overcome the highly mobile nature of language where meaning is created through socially constructed syntaxes which allow not simply representation to occur, but also silence, delay, and resistance in vocabulary to paradigms of meaning (say, in the work of poetics). The Freudian psychoanalytic model, too, works with representational notions, especially in its reading of dreams (*The Interpretation of Dreams*) and in the phenomenon of narcissism. Jacques Lacan goes further, grounding the ego's very formation on the initial phenomenon of reflection he calls "the mirror stage." One of the best analyses of the philosophy of reflection and the *imago* that I know of occurs in Mikkel Borch-Jacobsen's, *Lacan: The Absolute Master*, chapter 2, "The Statue Man." Rodolphe Gasché's *The Tain of the Mirror* is about the philosophy of reflection and "photology," and though longer than Borch-Jacobsen's work, is ground-breaking.

Wittgenstein, of course, uses the problem of pain to devastating effects in dismantling the representational view of language within *Philosophical Investigations*.

Further, certain cultures would find the notion of emotions being representative of 'inner states' startling. My experience, here, comes from discussions with Japanese students.

21. This move away from 'information-as-thing' (sui generis) is welcomed by many of the writers in the literature. In this study, for example, Robertson and Belkin (203), Robins and Webster (70), and Braman.

22. A practical example of the constructive power of systems, (as suggested by Harré (69)) upon social phenomenon is that of credit files. Harré asks the interesting question of the nature of the history that credit files create. Credit "histories" are interesting because, unlike narrative histories their range of interpretation is highly limited and their synthesis of non-systemic materials is nonexistent. They are 'ideal' histories, based on very selective quantitative materials. Their representational value serves the system of credit evaluation (based on purely binary criteria of debit or credit) and very poorly represents the social contexts of credit purchase, use, and default. Yet, of course, their power to represent people is immense and growing.

23. The vocabularies of both "systems" and "information" are notoriously slippery (Shrader counts 18 definitions of "information," many of them as states of being ("information as x")). In my view, there are two problems here: a methodological one and an institutional one.

Methodologically, the desire to define these terms is to attempt to recapture language within definition and representation. In reality, these terms don't need to be defined in order to be meaningful. Rather, each variance in the use of these terms identifies specific social constructions. As Wittgenstein argued, only rarely do social structures define meaning for language. Ordinarily, language shows the boundaries of social structures.

My second point is that the very desire to construct meaning for these terms is indicative of the institutional privilege of scientific rhetoric since the 17th and 18th centuries. Based on the model of the mathematical sciences, the criterium for a true and certain model of knowledge is the construction and stabilization of vocabulary and the maintenance of coherence within a system of language. (Not uncoincidentally, with the exception of the construction of neologisms, the criteria of vocabulary stability and internal coherence describes classical rhetoric as well.) As Machlup and Mansfield argue in regard to the metaphorical displacement of "information" from an engineering context to a more general one, the definitions of the quantitative sciences are often duplicated within other fields that are more qualitatively measured (and thus are more hermeneutic and 'uncertain') in order to render 'scientific' value to the latter fields (51 ff.). As Talcott Parsons said in 1938, the "professional type" is defined by "the pursuit and application of science" (quoted in Robins and Webster, 44). But further, as Samuel Weber argues, professionalism itself is defined by Western metaphysics and science, namely the definition and constructions of a 'field' of discourse through social and rhetorical devices (Weber, 48 ff.) and by the methodological question, "what is x?".

24. See my essay, "Commentary on 'Roy,' from Michael Amnasan's 'Unfair Play' ('Reserve' and 'Class')." *Mirage/Period(ical)* 2.

25. Avital Ronell has done a remarkable study of the telephone using Heideggerian and poststructural theory in *The Telephone Book*. See also Ronell's *Crack Wars* for the addictive properties of prescriptive electronic systems, and the metaphysical characteristics of Western culture which lay the ground for such addiction (and such technology). And see Ronell's article "Learning from Los Angeles; Haunted TV: Rodney King/Video/Trauma."

26. Not the least of these grounds is historical context. Speaking as a teacher of adults in a university setting for the past three years, I can readily testify to the near illiteracy of working adults in regard to written language older than fifty years. Symptomatic of a need for highly defined language (i.e., highly limited contexts for meaning) is their common complaint "what is the point?" Such a demand for rhetorical "points"—as supposedly context-free, self-evidential meaning within highly hermeneutic social contexts is chilling.

27. This is true, of course, according to classical Marxist theory, where labor and material become equivalent under capitalist production. The philosophical precedent for this, however, goes back to Aristotle's four causes, where labor and material are the means for the teleological fulfillment of the first cause (the "formal cause"—say, a blueprint for a house) within the last 'cause' (say, the house 'itself') (see Aristotle's *Metaphysics*).

28. Temporality is a very important concept within the formation of the ego for Freud from two perspectives. First in the original construction of the unconscious (and in *Totem and Taboo*, the primal origins of "social feelings" between men by a primal blow which is only known by the seeking to return to this missing origin (i.e., the Oedipal scene, or, earlier, the removal from the breast). Second, the construction of the ego is not only a compromise between Law and desire, but between what one thinks one can be (future) by what one thinks one was (past).

For Heidegger, temporality is foremost "ecstatic" (from the Greek, *ekstasis*) that is, it is not based on presence, on a series of nows, but is based on the displacement of a future by a past, and a past by a future, much as in the second sense of Freud, above, though the sense of the past ('tradition') is much stronger in Heidegger and leads to the phenomenon of repetition and the problematic of 'authenticity.' See *Being and Time*, especially section 74, "The Basic Condition of Historicality."

29. Robert Cooper writes,

> Post-industrialism tends toward a more systemised society in which people live increasingly commutual existences, bound together by their dependencies on organised systems which run on information. This entails the need to master "scale" or the distribution of information over space and time by means of new technological devices such as real-time computer information or new kinds of quantitative programming (Daniel Bell, *The Coming of the Post-industrial Society*). The general effect is to reduce differences by making everything instantaneously present and, therefore, unitary. (409)

Cooper goes on to argue that post-industrial systems favor performance over "size." I would disagree with this, because it is size which allows performance to be measured in terms of efficiency and speed. Size is the 'fixing' of scale, and the devaluation of the evaluative properties of space, much as serial temporality frames time within seriality.

Further, I would argue (and I don't think this would be contrary to the general tone of Cooper's article) that even as systems homogenize differences, they can also reply to specific differences within the framework of the system very effectively. Market economies 'grow' by this very ability to 'empower' a consumer or 'user' within the framework of (constructed) needs and wants. The presence of addictive formations is, of course, not simply a case of "constructed needs," but reaches back to historical formations which construct both the 'market' and the 'user.' We will argue this is the case with both "system" and "desire," as these terms develop in the early 19th century according to a certain notion of time.

30. See Derrida, *Given Time: I. Counterfeit Money*; David Wood, *The Deconstruction of Time*.

31. See Freud's letters to Wilhelm Fliess, collected in part in English under the title *The Origins of Psychoanalysis*.

32. Avital Ronell has certainly come as close as anyone in investigating the privileged relation of psychoanalytic discourse to systems theory. One of the more 'unconscious' writers on this topic, however, is Sara Fine, a professor at the University of Pittsburgh who has apparently performed studies for on psychological 'resistance' to technology. Her paper, "Terminal Paralysis" (in *Aspects of Automation*) presents a fascinating example of shared systems terminology between psychoanalysis, electrical engineering, and information science. Unfortunately, Fine's work is an example of the confusions that can occur in discourse by shared vocabularies, rather than an analysis of the assumptions which allow that 'sharing.'

Bibliography

Borch-Jacobsen, M. *Lacan: The Absolute Master*. Trans. D. Brick. Stanford University, 1991.

Braman, S. "Defining Information: An Approach for Policymakers." *Telecommunications Policy*, 13(3), September 1989. 233-242.

Buckland, M. *Information and Information Systems*. Greenwood Press, 1991.

Classification Research Group Bulletin, 1, November 1956. UMI Microfilm.

Classification Research Group Bulletin, 2, March-June 1957. UMI Microfilm

Coates, E. J. "CRG Proposals for a New General Classification." *Classification and Information Control: Papers Representing the Work of the Classification Research Group During 1960-1968*. The Library Association, 1969. 19-22.

Cooper, R. "Information, Communication and Organisation: A Post-Structural Revision." *The Journal of Mind and Behavior*, 8(3), summer 1987. 395-415.

Darnovsky, M. "Overhauling the Meaning Machines: An Interview with Donna Haraway." *Socialist Review*, 21(2), 1991. 65-84.

Day, R. H. "Systems, Information, and Economics." *The Study of Information: Interdisciplinary Messages*. Ed. F. Machlup & U. Mansfield. John Wiley and Sons, 1983. 619- 624.

Derrida, J. *Given Time: I. Counterfeit Money*. Trans. P. Kamuf. University of Chicago Press, 1992.

Derrida, J. *Of Grammatology*. Trans. G. Chakravorty Spivak. John Hopkins University, 1976.

Derrida, J. "Ousia and Gramme: Notes on a Note from *Being and Time*." *Margins of Philosophy*. Trans. A. Bass. University of Chicago, 1982.

Derrida, J., T. Pepper, E. Esch & T. Keenan. "Sendoffs." *Yale French Studies*, 77, 1990. 7-43.

Fine, S. "Aspects of Automation." in *Human Aspect of Library Automation: Helping Staff and Patrons Cope: Papers presented at the 1985 Clinic on Library Applications of Data Processing*, April 14-16, 1985.

Foucault, M. *The Order of Things: An Archaeology of the Human Sciences*. Random House, 1973.

Fremery, W. de. *Cats, Carpenters, and Accountants: Bibliographical Foundations of Information Science*. MIT Press, 2024.

Freud, S. *The Interpretation of Dreams*. Trans. J. Strachey. Avon Books, 1965.

Freud, S. *Totem and Taboo*. Trans. J. Strachey. W.W. Norton and Co., 1989.

Gasché, R. *Tain of the Mirror: Derrida and the Philosophy of Reflection*. Harvard University Press, 1986.

Gates, Jr., H. L. *"Race," Writing, and Difference*. The University of Chicago, 1986.

Haraway, D. "A Manifesto for Cyborgs: Science, Technology, and Socialist Feminism in the 1980s." *Socialist Review*, 15(2), 1985. 65-107.

Harré, R. *Personal Being: A Theory of Individual Psychology*. Harvard University, 1984.

Hegel, G.W. F. *The Phenomenology of Spirit*. Trans. A.V. Miller. Oxford University Press, 1977.

Heidegger, M. *Being and Time*. Trans. J. Macquarrie & E. Robinson. Harper and Row, 1962.

Heidegger, M. *The Concept of Time*. Trans. W. McNeill. Blackwell, 1992.

Heidegger, M. "The End of Philosophy and the Task of Thinking." Trans. J. Stambaugh. *Basic Writings*. Ed. D. F. Krell. Harper and Row, 1977. 373-392.

Heidegger, M. "On the Essence of Truth." Trans. J. Sallis. *Basic Writings*. Ed. D. F. Krell. Harper and Row, 1977. 113-142.

Heidegger, M. *Schelling's Treatise on the Essence of Human Freedom*. Trans. J. Stambaugh. Ohio University Press, 1985.

Heidegger, M. "What is Metaphysics?" Trans. D. F. Krell. *Basic Writings*. Ed. D. F. Krell. Harper and Row, 1977. 91-112.

Kant, I. *Critique of Judgment*. Trans. W. S. Pluhar. Hackett Publishing, 1987.

Langlois, R. N. "On the Reception of Noise: A Rejoiner." *The Study of Information: Interdisciplinary Messages*. Ed. F. Machlup & U. Mansfield. John Wiley and Sons, 1983. 631-640.

Lovejoy, A. O. *The Great Chain of Being: The Study of the History of an Idea*. Harper and Row, 1960.

Lyotard, J.-F. *The Inhuman*. Stanford University, 1991.

Lyotard, J.-F. *The Postmodern Condition: A Report on Knowledge*. Trans. G. Bennington & B. Massumi. University of Minnesota, 1984.

Machlup, F. "Semantic Quirks in Studies of Information." *The Study of Information: Interdisciplinary Messages*. Ed. F. Machlup & U. Mansfield. John Wiley and Sons, 1983. 641-672.

Machlup, F. & U. Mansfield. "Cultural Diversity in Studies of Information." *The Study of Information: Interdisciplinary Messages*. Ed. F. Machlup & U. Mansfield. John Wiley and Sons, 1983. 3-56.

Meadow, C. T. *Text Information Retrieval Systems*. Harcourt, Brace, Jovanovich, 1992.

Nancy, J.-L. "'Eating Well,' or the Calculation of the Subject: An Interview with Jacques Derrida." *Who Comes After the Subject?* Trans. P. Connor & A. Ronell. 1991. 96-119.

Nancy, J.-L. *The Inoperative Community*. Ed. P. Connor. University of Minnesota, 1991.

Nancy, J.-L. "Telling the Tree: Narrative Representation and the study of Evolutionary History." *Biology and Philosophy*, 7, 1992. 135-160.

Nancy, J.-L. *Who Comes After the Subject?* Ed. E. Cadava, P. Connor, J.-L. Nancy. Routledge, 1991.

O'Hara, R. J. "Representations of the Natural System in the Nineteenth Century." *Biology and Philosophy.* 6, 1991. 255-274.

Paton, R. C. "Towards a Metaphorical Biology." *Biology and Philosophy*, 7, 1992. 279–94.

Ranganathan, S. R. *Philosophy of Library Classification.* Ejnar Munksgaard, 1951.

Ranganathan, S. R. *Prolegomena to Library Classification.* The Library House, 1957.

Reddy, M. J. "The Conduit Metaphor—A Case of Frame Conflict in Our Language About Language." *Metaphor and Thought.* Ed. A. Ortony. Cambridge University, 1978.

Robertson, S. E. & N. J. Belkin. "Information Science and the Phenomenon of Information." *Journal of the American Society for Information Science,* 27(4), 1976. 197-204.

Robins, K. & F. Webster. "Cybernetic Capitalism: Information, Technology, Everyday Life." *The Political Economy of Information.* Ed. V. Mosco & J. Wasco. University of Wisconsin, 1988. 44-73.

Ronell, A. *Crack Wars.* University of Nebraska, 1992.

Ronell, A. "Learning from Los Angeles: Haunted TV: Rodney King/Video/Trauma." *Artforum*, 30(1), September 1992. 70-73.

Ronell, A. *The Telephone Book: Technology, Schizophrenia, Electric Speech.* University of Nebraska, 1989.

Ross, A. "Getting the Future We Deserve." *Socialist Review*, 21, 1991. 125-150.

Sayers, W. C. B. *A Manual of Classification for Librarians and Bibliographers.* Coptic House, Grafton and Co., 1926.

Schrader, A. M. "In Search of a Name: Information Science and its Conceptual Antecedents." *Library and Information Science Research*, 6(3), July-September 1984. 227-271.

Tomlinson, H. "Concepts Within Politics." *Classification and Information Control: Papers Representing the Work of the Classification Research Group During 1960-1968.* The Library Association, 1969. 68-72.

Tomlinson, H. "Problems Arising From First GCS Papers." *Classification and Information Control: Papers Representing the Work of the Classification Research Group During 1960-1968.* The Library Association, 1969. 73-80.

Weber, S. "The Vaulted Eye: Remarks on Knowledge and Professionalism." *Reading the Archives: On Texts and Institutions. Yale French Studies*, 77, 1990. 44-60.

Wittgenstein, L. *Philosophical Investigations.* Basil Blackwell, 1976.

Wood, D. *The Deconstruction of Time.* Atlantic Humanities Press International, 1989.

Animal Songs
Translation, Community, The Question of the 'Animal:' In-formation

As for me, I talk about the philosopher, but I am not simply a philosopher.... It is in this strategic context that on occasion I have spoken of philosophy's usefulness in translating or deciphering a number of things, such as what goes on in the media, and so on.

Jacques Derrida, "Roundtable on Translation"

But in regard to the shrill voice, the peculiarity is—not that they [the witnesses] disagreed—but that, while an Italian, an Englishman, a Spaniard, a Hollander, and a Frenchman attempted to describe it, each one spoke of it as that of a foreigner. Each is sure that it was not the voice of one of his countrymen. Each likens it—not to the voice of an individual of any nation with whose language he is conversant—but the converse. The Frenchman supposes it the voice of a Spaniard, and 'might have distinguished some words had he been acquainted with the Spanish.' The Dutchman maintains it to have been that of a Frenchman; but we find it stated that 'not understanding French this witness was examined through an interpreter.' The Englishman thinks it the voice of a German, and 'does not understand German.' The Spaniard 'is sure' that was that of an Englishman, but 'judges by the intonation' altogether, 'as he has not knowledge of the English.' The Italian believes it the voice of a Russian, but 'has never conversed with a native of Russia.'... Now, how strangely unusual must that voice have really been, about which such testimony as this could have been elicited!

Edgar Allen Poe, "The Murders in the Rue Morgue," quoted in Fritz Gutbrodt, "Poedelaire: Translation and the Volatility of the Letter"

Preface

What follows constitutes a reading of community according to progressively deterritorialized readings of the term "information." This latter term mobilizes various epistemic "assemblages" or "machines" (as Deleuze and Guattari might call such structures) that may be described by various relations to metaphor: information as exchange, reproduction, and presence and representation; information as flow; information as the result of the site of metaphor itself. These three positions correspond to three relations toward reading alterity: that of pure presence, that of the play and construction of presence and absence in discursive formations, and that of the experience of alterity. How we think of community, I would argue, is a question of how we read alterity.

Supposing this "age" of "information," it is therefore imperative to ask how we are willing to think the relation of information to alterity. In terms of the philosophy of presence, positive definitions of information prove to follow representative claims of knowledge. "Information," here, elicits claims of correspondence truth, positive representation, systemic reproduction, certainty, and the communicative "exchange" of meaning in an ideal economy of language. In terms of discursive formations, "information" connotes economic analyses of the formation of meaning within discourses of power, as well as the "flow" of meaning across surfaces, planes, or assemblages of continuities. Economic analyses of information may follow the work of Michel Foucault in trying to understand the historical forms through which meaning is produced as "useful" or "non-useful" (among other categories). The emphasis here is upon the logics of oppression which give certain values to terms and deny it to others, and which regulate and deregulate economies of values. Analyses of information "flow" may follow the work of Deleuze and Guattari in understanding "information" as the flow and the products of cultural assemblages (composed by both language and actions) in their construction as surfaces of meaning, their interconnections as zones of meaning, and in terms of reified discourses and identities. Deleuze and Guattari's works are useful in attempting to think the relation between technology and humans in a way that deterritorializes dialectical logics and emphasizes cybernetic relations. Their works are also useful, as I will argue in the third chapter, in attempting to think the relation of "information" to the question of the "animal." Lastly, we may wish to think the term "information" at the limits of the informed surface of discourse, that is, in terms of an alterity that cannot be breached—that of finitude. This is to say, in the event which I will mark as "in-(>)forming," at the site of the joint or hinge of originary *différance*. Such a site constitutes not so much the reversal of Deleuze and Guattari's radical critique, but rather a thinking of the joining of beings in terms of the philosophy of presence—that is, in terms of its failure. Where Deleuze and Guattari deterritorialize presence to such a point that presence becomes a matter of "zones," a destructive (Heidegger) or deconstructive (Derrida) critique of presence remains wary of Nietzsche's example in privileging becoming over being (according to Heidegger, an inverted Platonism).

Previously, originating from a tradition of communication theory, the "use" of information was measured according to conduit models of language and correspondence criteria for truth. These models of presence, re-presentation, and systemic reproduction are no longer adequate bases with which to think "information." This is due to many causes, not the least being both the end of modern utopias and the inability of positive science to ground itself. Practically speaking, the term connotes wider social and political expectations than was the case when Claude Shannon used the word to denote the transfer of electrical impulses. Nor can the problem of the "use" of information be restricted to what has previously been thought through "pragmatic" or "communicational" theories of regulated exchange (I have in mind here the work of Rorty on the one hand, and Habermas and Apel on the other). If "information" can no longer simply denote electrical transfer, much less a re-presentation of so-called "datum," it also can no longer uncritically refer to the appearance of "truth" through ghostly or rhetorical stabilizing contexts of "reason." Following the work of both Samuel Weber in critical theory and Patrick Wilson in information studies, I would like to propose that thinking the "pragmatic" in regard to "information" must be done not only in terms of conditions of use, but in terms of conditions of "failure" and in terms of origin and difference. The term "information" now largely competes with "knowledge" in both public and professional lexicons, and as such, "information" needs to be thought in terms of cultural theory and in terms of a relation toward truth. That is to say, "information" needs to be thought in terms of social and cultural theory, and also, in terms of epistemology, ontology, and other sub-disciplines of philosophy. This is not a demand we place upon some rather vague concept that is the referent for the term "information." This is a demand that the term calls out to us by its very instability of reference and by ever wider and ever more pressing social forces that attempt to define this term according to some particular assemblage of values and use. (As one example: the concept of the "information age" which ties "information" into a modernist reading of history in terms of succession and progress.)

In order to engage in critical study, the information profession must almost resist the forces of its own professionalization in the sciences and in the modern form of the university.[1] That is to say, it must resist the ideal reification of "information" as an exclusive object of study, and instead, be willing to think the term in its historical location—that is, a term which is literally everywhere across the postmodern landscape. Given the breakdown of universal (meta-)narratives, "information profession" designates less a meta-site for disciplinary authority over "information," and more a critical site between meta-discourses (or "discursive fields") in their reconstruction under postmodernism. Similar to "knowledge" in the 18th century and "history" in the 19th, "information" designates the organization and practice of meaning under current social, political, cultural, and economic conditions, as well as the history and logic of these conditions' organization and practice. These "conditions" cannot exhaust the term, nor should these categories be exhaustive sites for analyzing the term. "Information" has histories and logics which give to these "conditions" their configuration and link them with the term "information." This is to say, "information" must not be understood only synchronically, but diachronically as well, without clear delineations separating the two realms of analyses in terms of the empiricism of the "social sciences" and the conceptual/historical analyses of the "humanities." The critical study of "information" as a social, political, cultural, and economic term demands its analysis in terms of philosophy. None of these "fields" or "conditions" can ignore their site of departure in philosophy; this is especially true as these terms designate scientific fields of analysis. This is not to say that the sciences are reducible to the history of philosophy or to the discipline of philosophy, but rather that what we today call 'the sciences' respond to philosophical questions that allow both philosophy and the sciences to proceed. (In its most basic form, the question is, 'what is the nature of reality,' or 'what is...'.)[2] The "in-betweenness" of the term "information"—its very indetermination—involves all the sciences; that is to say, "information," even in its specialized meanings, is a philosophical term that is of utmost importance to us who use it. This is to say that the term is interdisciplinary for those of us in, or under, Western culture at this time. "Interdisciplinary" not in the sense of that which may be borrowed or exchanged between disciplines, but as the between itself which comes to color the cultural understanding and use of all scientific disciplines. The determination of "information" as promoting this or that assemblage of capital or 'pragmatic' conditions is a problem to us now, whether we like it or not.

Professionalization forces upon us the ethical demand of being accountable for the capitalization of vocabulary within the world. Critically understanding the capitalization of "information" and resisting the reification of this term by any single economy is the responsibility of those who refer to themselves as "information professionals" today. Any other claim for this latter term is a claim made within a highly class-isolated modernism, or, within a notion of information technology whose claims upon the term "information" are narrowly limited to a by-gone era, but which profits by the passing of this very same era.

"Me, a name, I call myself.... ":: Translation

> To grasp the genuine relationship between an original and a translation requires an investigation analogous to the argumentation by which a critique of cognition would have to prove the impossibility of an image theory. There is a matter of showing that in cognition there could be no objectivity, not even a claim to it, if it dealt with images or reality; here it can be demonstrated that no translation would be possible if in its ultimate essence it strove for the likeness to the original. For in its afterlife—which could not be called that if it were not a transformation and a renewal of something living—the original undergoes a change.... Translation is so far removed from being the sterile equation of two dead languages that of all literary forms it is the one charged with the special mission of watching over the maturing process of the original language and the birth pangs of its own.
>
> Walter Benjamin, "The Task of the Translator"

Translation and the Double Bind

Benjamin's quote begins our discussion because it launches the question of translation into an im-possible zone: that of the constitution of an original message. Benjamin's organic claims in this quote ("afterlife," "something living" (72)) are, he tells us, not simply metaphors, but they constitute the empirical conditions of a work 'in' translation:

namely, that it exceed whatever may be thought of as its original conditions of meaning by the fact of its repetitive transformations. For Benjamin, as for Derrida, the archetype of such originary texts are sacred texts, which begin and end in translation. The text itself is understood as the *logos* of that which is beyond finite reason, and in the Judeo-Christian tradition every sacred text claims itself as a transformation, even within the written tradition (hence Luther's justification of translating the Bible *for* the German people).[3] (Nor must we must forget that the two earliest canonical Christian gospels (Mark and Matthew) claim to be a new translation of God's word to the Jewish people, and that the latter two gospels, as well as the early church's pronouncements, define themselves against Gnosticism by a translation of Hellenism.)

As Benjamin remarks in regard to Friedrich Hölderlin's translations, especially that of Sophocles, however, such repetition marks a sublimity in the original text as much as it fails to give the illusion of literalism, and in as much it joins with the original in marking and remarking the "saying" of a text, particularly a literary text (70, 81-82). This is to say that the success of Hölderlin's translation lies not in the transportation of language, but in conditions of transmission which allow a continual iteration of the original to develop out of an estranged language. These conditions of transmission lie within what Derrida has called a "double bind": namely, the demand of the text: "translate me... don't translate me."[4]

In his text, "Des Tours de Babel," Derrida reads this double bind in terms of the story of Babel and in terms of the proper name. As Derrida narrates the story, the people of Shem built a tower to speak in the name of God. God's punishment for this act of pride was to make them speak of him in the name of Babel—literally, "Confusion." God's proper name is thus, "Confusion," a proper name that is also a common noun. God's name is translated within discursive economies as "confusion," but 'in-itself' it defies translation (how does one translate the condition and the sending of all translation: "confusion"?). The proper name is thus sent out, but also holds something in reserve. Its singularity and exposure are manifested in terms of its translation, but this manifestation does not give it its being, but rather, in the very 'failure' of translation marks what is held in reserve.

For Benjamin, not all texts call for translation. Translation is a demand or a "call" (70) put out by the original to which we respond. The relay of translation is put out by a question for which an answer is not immediate. Whether the posing of the original is answered or not, the demand of the original remains because of the alterity which composes it. Such reserve defeats notions of translation as systemic reproduction or as a repetition of the "Same." In Blanchot's terms, such a posing of the 'other' before us does not occur in the systemic nature of rumor or opinion where question and answer form a circle of response which may have nothing to do with the formation of meaning, but rather with sociability or agreement.[5] Authenticity is marked in the translation not as a recoverable site for understanding and 'information'(*qua* transferable communication), but rather by an excess which is the ineffable sum of all the translations (or to put it another way, the sum of all translations points to an excess beyond their sum). For Benjamin, "pure language" is the excess and reserve of all languages, in a non-exhaustible 'summation.' As Derrida argues from Benjamin, "pure language" is the saying of language itself.

How is language said? How does translation constitute the saying of language which is forgotten? For Benjamin, translation addresses some sense of authentic trauma. Benjamin notes that if we were to restrict such significant events "exclusively to man,"

> One might, for example, speak of an unforgettable life or moment even if all men had forgotten it. If the nature of such a life or moment required that it be unforgotten, that predicate would not imply a falsehood but merely a claim not fulfilled by men, and probably also a reference to a realm in which it *is* fulfilled: God's remembrance. Analogously, the translatability of linguistic creations ought to be considered even if men should prove unable to translate them. (70)

Benjamin's reading of translation, as an effort of recuperation of the impossible meaning of the original extends here to the problem of recuperating the essence of language. Such an activity can only take place through languages, but in so doing, within the logic of the double bind, must appeal to an original which remains as the condition of language(s). This desire to recuperate meaning itself is marked in Hegel's philosophy by the movements of Spirit (*Geist*) toward Absolute Being, and it is the necessary groundwork for any positive theory of translation and universal transmission. If, however, the transmission of language itself cannot be guaranteed, then no parts of it can be guaranteed. It is the im-possibility of language itself which sends the desire of translation to absolutely re-present the other, and yet which marks translation's 'failure' to re-present the original. Derrida marks this project of recuperation beginning in language as the origin of desire, and in its double bind, it constitutes an irreducible aporia to presence which cannot be resolved ("Roundtable," 116).

As Derrida notes, in Benjamin's work poetry is understood in terms of the sacred ("Roundtable," 148). Poetry marks the sacred in the way that translation marks the original, even though the original may have been forgotten. This analogy between poetry and translation occurs, not only because poetry is said to be untranslatable, but because poetry is translation itself as far as it attempts to constitute in (a) language that which exceeds (a) language. Translation and poetry differ only in regard to the form of the other. Generally, the form of the other in translation is that of textuality; in poetry, that of the world. However, as Benjamin indicates in the quote with which we began this chapter, not only 'life,' but 'individuals' and 'texts' are inscribed in-common in the Western tradition according to organic metaphors. Traditionally, organic metaphors give their terms qualities such as autonomy and absolute presence, and subsequently, read translation as re-presentation. Benjamin's counter-reading of translation, however, allows us to read these terms according to the 'failure' of translation, and to draw epistemological and ontological parallels out of textual claims. These parallels to the phenomenon of language occur within the tradition itself, as we noted in the story of Babel. *Logos*, within the Western Judeo-Christian tradition unmistakably refers not only to language, but to community and knowledge as well. As far as "poetry" is made up of language, meaning, and truth, it constitutes a founding site for reading the meaning of human being in terms of language, political being, and knowledge. As constituting, poetry can also be read as a limit to representation, Western philosophical thinking, and further, what we commonly call 'information' (again, understood strictly in terms of communicational representation), as these constitute culture-specific traditions of reading, language, meaning, and truth. Poetry is the naming of the indetermination of these terms, and the point at which these terms can be contested, not only in terms of their universal or global claims over human being, but in terms of their displacement and reorientation.[6] Thus, not only Benjamin, but also Derrida, and even Heidegger concur in reading *poiesis* as the originating difference of representational thinking.

The point at which translation fails to translate is, for Benjamin, the site at which languages are in-common in regard to things, including the language of the original. As Benjamin explains, the words *Brot* and *pain* in German and French have a similar ideal extension, but their connotations construct a different notion of the object in each language (Benjamin, 74). In a Kantian manner, however, no things can be posited as 'objects' outside of this linguistic understanding, unless, of course, such objects be posited as the ideal ends of science or in the mind of God. The "anasemic" origins of language (the term comes from the psychoanalyst Nicolas Abraham's text "The Shell and the Kernel") are thus marked in this unending complimentarity of languages that never end. "Anasemic origins" means, in this case, the 'non-linguistic' origins for language, or rather, how language as representation has its origin in an irreducible difference in the between of 'thing' and representation. In terms of translation, "anasemic origins" refers not only to the "untranslatable" elements of the original which both demand and 'challenge' translations, but to the distance that original has to itself. Rodolphe Gasché succinctly describes the non-identity of the original in a question for Jacques Derrida in "Roundtable on Translation":

> If, as you have indeed shown in "Fors," any translation, of whatever sort, has its starting point in the impossible translation of each language's asemic kernel—a kernel that is obviously nonidentical and non-present to itself—does translation leave it intact as an unrepresentable kernel or, on the contrary, does every translation only help to better displace and better defer the absolute nonpresence of this kernel itself? Or to put it still more simply, isn't translation the operator of différance, deferring and differing that which makes it possible? And in this case, shouldn't we instead take up the problem again of the conditions of possibility of any translation and of its effect, namely, différance? (114)

Gasché, in the above, points back to the problem of an irreducible difference in translation which is both the source for translation and is the 'other' which the language of 'man' must overcome according to the humanist tradition in order to reach, or equal, God. As we have mentioned, such a difference is marked by a double bind—"translate/don't [or rather, "can't"] translate"—which is the condition of language as representation. This *"différance"*—a difference not of plural identities, but of a command which both demands its own closure and endlessly defers such closure (hence, one reading of Derrida's *"différance"*[7]), resulting in multiple readings of the original, tied to the original ("difference" in terms of an obligation or debt to an original *"différance"*)—is the demand of the original upon translation.

The "original," however, is marked by an endless series of cuts and schisms which defy its self-identity (in terms of auto-presentation). In Benjamin's work, as in Derrida's, not only can the translation fail to re-present an original, but it fails primarily because of the inability of any language or text to represent *itself* as that of a closed and absolute presence that needs merely to be duplicated. Benjamin lays forth the conditions for translation—or the im-possibility of translation—in terms of time and the difference of historical reception:

> Even words with fixed meaning can undergo a maturing process. The obvious tendency of a writer's literary style may in time wither away, only to give rise to immanent tendencies in the literary creation. What sounded fresh once may sound hackneyed later; what was once current may someday sound quaint. (73)

As many have pointed out, the very title of Derrida's "Des Tours de Babel" is "untranslatable"—not only into English, but into French as well.[8] The "drifting" of meaning in literary texts is a well-known phenomenon. According to Ferdinand de Saussure, in his *Course in General Linguistics*, meaning does not originate in simple representation, but rather, meaning is determined within an economy of differences. The determination of any language as a single economy—even an economy of itself (French as French, English as English, etc.)—is impossible because of both the historical formation of a language (or a text) from 'other' languages and because of synchronic conditions of reception. As to the former, historical conditions demand that no language can maintain a vocabulary as strictly its own nor that speakers belong to a single order of language. As to the latter, as Deleuze and Guattari argue, the more 'major' a language is said to be, the more we are saying that it is composed of 'minor' languages which far exceed the ability for there to be a normative 'major' language. Within the law of the double bind, 'English,' as the original, is composed of differences which compose 'English' beyond the possibility of a 'Standard' language of 'English.' The original is cut and recut according to 'borrowings' from other languages which promote the inability for any language to be strictly duplicated—even in relation to itself, that is, in regard to its own self-representation. (As in the problem of Baudelaire's translation of Poe's "Purloined Letter," how is an American short story situated in France to be translated into French while preserving the foreignness of 'France' in Poe's story?) Not only do the meanings of styles and words change in time, but changes in social grammars lead to temporary meaning stabilization only through an incredible number of dialogues among speakers. The stabilization of meaning toward a utopia of translation requires tremendous powers of social control operating over long periods of time. Once a "standard" language is achieved, however, such ideologies, or prejudices of language, need no longer account for either empirical changes, other languages, or even speakers themselves. Language, here, ceases to be an event, and instead becomes a spectacle that must maintain its system of presence through semiotic, as well as physical repression and institutions of repression.

Identity

As mentioned earlier, the problem of translation extends within the Western tradition to problems of community, and thus to problems of cultural identity. Fidelity and faithful reproduction are goals not only of absolute translation, but also of national fascisms, and they depend on the erasure of translation as transformative. What must not be thought in questions of identity in the West is the *inability* of identity to represent itself to the point of closure (that is, what must not be thought is the double bind of representation). Every positing of what 'one is' means a division in the speaking subject because what cannot be included in the representation is the act of positing, itself. This *différance* between the person and the discourses of identity within which the person situates its being is forgotten in a forgetting of the relation between Being and time. Further, the discourses of identity forget their own historicity *within the speaking, rather than within the discourse of identity itself.* That someone feels the pressure to identify him or her 'self' as 'this' or 'that' self is historically indicative of a social violence forcing a person to identify him or her 'self' as some Same-being through a reified, authenticating past. Within the Western tradition, the absolute translation of self from some past origin is necessary when that self is invalidated as a singularity with not only one, but multiple histories which are not simply 'his' or 'hers' but shared in different degrees, modes, and moods of specificity. But this relation of *claiming* an identity, that is, as offering an identity as a thesis for what one is—as a capitalization of the singularity of historical

Being, and as an order for becoming in a manner of defeating the rhizomic nature of history and Being—is inherent to the violence of Western metaphysical understandings. The law of the "trans"—the above or through (in regard to trans-lation, trans-formation, transportation, and most of all, trans-mission) must be rethought in terms of the irreducible *différance* of all representations. This demands a thinking of language at its limits—at the *différance* of translation—rather than within representational orders. Jean Luc-Nancy, in discussing the meaning of the terms "Chicano"/"Chicana" points to a 'people' who are a people by means of the historicity of their identity in terms of both language and 'blood'; that is, are a people not by their gathering within a 'true' history or a 'race,' but rather, by having had traced upon their singular bodies the violence of certain, specific histories, both now and in the past:

> Language holds the social bond, but it holds it at the limit, on the limit of unravelling. Language itself is always at the limit, always at its own breaking point. But with that, unbound, sprung from its course, it crosses its own limits, back and forth, underlining them and passing over them. "Americans," "Chicanos," that much is comprehensible. It is quite comprehensible, too much so, and not enough, at the same time.
>
> All of which doesn't mean much. It only opens up the indefinite, multiple, criss-crossed, divided, broken series of mestizaje, or 'mis-weavings,' of the cut, of uncountable cuts. Couplings and cuts. Every "people" is made up of them—assembled/cut. What people is not?...
>
> But the birth of your people, its incessant birth and rebirth up to today—when you come into the *world*, into this one world to which we are all continuously arriving—your birth will not be the return to myth. It will be, it is already, the foundation of that which has neither a pure foundation nor an identifiable origin: of that Aztlan which you *are*, arriving from yourselves, beheaded suns. The foundation is the cut.
>
> ("Soleil cou coupé" ("Beheaded Sun"), 44)

The inability of *logos* to be capitalized by any one language, thesis, form, or head-ing *(cap)*, and "pure language" to be the unclosed complementarity of all overlapping and incomplete languages, projects both a heterogeneity and a specificity over community and personal identity. Since the original cannot be constituted as an absolute presence it cannot be claimed, recuperated, or identified within terms of a single identity. On the other hand, a response to an original signifies a debt of reply.

In the Western tradition, the West arrives back to itself not by the citation of its multiple cuts, but through the colonialism of those cuts as multiple examples of the history of the Same—namely, its history or to say the same, 'world history.' The West translates its origins in terms of the Same, and thus, as Derrida argues in *The Other Heading (L'autre cap)*, the West finds its national home through a gathering inter-multi-nationalism. The original thus translates itself in terms of an other which gains an identity in terms of how much it comes to formally resemble the presence which the original sees itself as. Berman argues that for Goethe, German national *Bildung* was achieved by claiming a peculiar *internationalism* of the German people, especially in terms of translation.[10] This capitalization of German *Kulture* through a dialectical logic of formation (*Bildung*) fails to think the cuts which makes up its origin in terms of a specific historical Being, a series of cuts which cannot translate the other in terms of being an *example* of a unitary origin. Indeed, as Nancy suggests, the original is not simply constituted by its translations or repetitions, but these repetitions can only repeat because of the countless rhizomes of difference which make up the original and thus rupture any 'true' translation. Origin is not a project of self-projection (and thus translation is not the forming of an origin by repetition of the Same), but origins have an historical, rather than a mythical, specificity. Their assemblages are those of cuts which extend into the past and into the future. It is not simply that translations 'make' the 'original,' but rather, that translations respond to an alterity, an endless string of differences which makes up origination.

Translation must, therefore, be spoken of in terms of a reply to alterity, not as the original is absolutely present, but rather as it is a *singular* or *queer* (*singulier*) exposure of a being in terms of a history that exceeds it. The gathering of the original is not in the mode of recuperation, but in the loss of a heading. This loss of teleological determination—the indeterminacy of poetry in regard to the scale by which its meaning should be measured—situates the original as an exposure to the limits of language and 'what is.' Therefore, the return which translation argues for, in its essential im-possibility, is a return to its own difference: in the common form of Babel, or that is to say, in the specificity of confusion and freedom.

Cultural identity, in its least transcendental form, is a return to a specific relation of identity to alterity and is thus a seeking of the *event* of freedom (the event of translation) through a critical working through of the forms of metaphysical 'origins' thrust upon a given person. Put simply: at its least metaphysical, cultural identity is a *project* of working through prejudice and representative formations of identity until the social violence of metaphysical identification is no more.

Though we can easily enough think the logical form of an event of freedom, such a return, in all its worldly specificity, is made more difficult when one is always already assigned an alien otherness to an origin of presence (in terms of being-an-example-of or being-the-labor-for). *The experience of alterity is not the same as the experience of marginality*. The liberal identification of alterity and repression purposefully confuses an alienation *in regard to law* with an alienation *by law*. This identification disallows freedom as event and defines freedom as lack of repression. Freedom is, however, not the disappearance of this or that repression, but the experience of the condition of law in general. The *angst* of alienation may indeed, from one angle, be the same in both cases, but the experience of freedom is not. *Différance* cannot be reduced to liberal difference. Translation, as the commonality of the cut, requires a thinking beyond the experience of the 'pro and con,' 'winners and losers,' as well as beyond the gathering internationalism of liberal thought and the forgetting of law in the 'trans' of trans-missions.

In the next chapter, we will attempt to think the law of the 'information era' as the self-appointed destination of global capitalization.

"On a clear day, you can see forever":: Postmodern/Post-apocalypse

Capitalizing Information

The concept of an electronic democracy, which acquires in Western countries the form of both a national and transnational language, depends not only on the domination of global technological standards but upon idealist notions of the term "information." The rhetoric of global emancipation and "communication" are so dominant in both popular and professional discussions of the future of information and community that it would be both impossible and unnecessary to attribute such claims to any one article, book, individual, or groups of individuals. In his fine article, "Towards an Electronic Democracy," Giovanni Cesareo asks if such claims are works of futurology or of seduction (71). If such claims are in fact seductive, it would be necessary to delineate the already assumed truths which seduce us into thinking electronic democracy and virtual community as the truths of the future. And it would be necessary not only to think the limitations of these truths in terms of their own claims, but to think outside these truths, in terms of what is repressed by the 'imminent' self-evidence of the future.

The term 'information,' when understood as self-representational atomic units of meaning, forms the backbone for the electronic democracy. Along the lines of Western liberal democratic theory, the claim is made that 'information' is composed of factual representations which must, in an electronic democracy, be released to a 'virtual community' of individual voices who will then utilize the electronic system to assert their own presence and will conduct their own liberation through such information. The machinery of (electronic) democracy thus rests on two main assumptions: (1) that liberation is possible by the consumption of all relevant facts (*qua* 'information'), and (2) politics is the presence of an individual (indivisible) voice in the ex-pression and ex-pulsion of previously consumed (and then internally judged, processed, or digested) facts.

Putting aside the not inconsequential problems of overload and relevance, the first assumption is naive in that it overly simplifies the nature of meaning in language. First of course, language does not simply represent 'objective' conditions of the world. Such positivism was long ago abandoned in the physical sciences. 'Evidence' does not "speak by itself," but instead, "speaks" because of rhetoric and discourse which give it functions of representation. The problem of factuality is discursive, and the problem of facticity may well be the condition of returning to a problem rather than of 'clearing it up.' Second, even if we were to think of information in terms of usefulness (rather than exclusively as representational 'facts'), we are left with the problem of what would constitute a useful 'piece' of information. Would such data be 'raw' or thoroughly 'cooked' in order to meet conditions of consumption and oral expulsion? If 'raw' (or 'atomic'), then how could many types of statistics be utilized by non-experts (not to say illiterates)?

Would not raw data consumption be severely taxed by conditions of overload (indigestion? clogging of the arteries of thought or speech)? Is it possible to reduce useful information to statistic-like units? As Cesareo notes, "processed" data are "richer" but they tend to assume narrower discursive uses (78).

But the notion that we consume (indeed, digest) knowledge, information, etc. (—whether raw or processed, thin or rich—), is a misleading metaphor. Rather, we circulate with 'facts' in discourses of information and knowledge, and we are responsible for the continuance and change of such circulation with our language acts. "Responsible" here means that we *respond* to language, with language, and part of our critical responsibility is to respond to this response itself—a response which is engaged within an alterity that exceeds any language. Ethically, this means that we cannot always take refuge in a response that denies language (such as that of science). This is particularly important when faced with the metaphors of quantitative science as applied to the social world, such as "data" and "atomic" units of meaning. The language of the world is not reducible to scientific laws, because there is no such entity as the 'language of the world' (and thus, no such law), and because the usefulness of language in the world is not due to its correspondence with objective things, but rather, to its ability to make things happen. Such 'making things happen' refers not only to prescriptive uses of language, but to a 'pragmatic' reply to things which marks the appropriation of language. It is necessary to think not only the in-form-ed nature of information in regard to the *pragma*, but the informing of things which allow things to "happen" in language as the *event* of language. We must account for information in terms of not only representation, but poetics and the advent of science. This means that 'information' can no longer avoid the indeterminate in thinking its *pragma*. It means that in thinking language and *pragma* we must discuss both 'use' and the traditionally 'useless.'

It is simplistic to think that every person can equally 'make things happen' in language, or that 'each' is somehow outside of language or within a language. These fallacies correspond to the notion that language refers to 'raw' presences of things, and that all languages are reducible to a single language that is 'out there,' as consumable and expulsive as a piece of meat—as the 'animal.' Even Wittgenstein's notion of the 'language game,' if understood in a sense of hidden normative rules for language use, falls victim to this. Specialized languages, for example, 'contain' specialists in the sense that specialists utilize a 'scientific' language toward a certain assumption of what that language can do. This repetition of the Same in science cannot lie within the language, but neither does it lie outside of it. This repetition patrols a language as it creates a futurity for the language and the field. At the same time, such a language is a response to a question that lies outside of it. What propels the sciences in their distancing from philosophy is the very question of philosophy: 'what is the nature of reality?' In turn, their distancing is the archetypal philosophical response for answering the call of the real. The assumption of what science can do is rooted in the assumptions of philosophy and the terms in which we commonly think truth—that is, in terms of a finding out. That is to say, the language of the specialized sciences lies outside of the sciences, in the sense that the question of philosophy lies 'outside' of the discipline of philosophy. What lies outside philosophy is a call which is not an assumption since the reply never answers it in a teleological manner. In this way, philosophy obviously fails its own teleological criteria for truth. But in so 'failing' to answer the philosophical question, the question becomes more important, and its answering assumes a variety of discourses.

"Communicational" communities, such as those issuing from the Enlightenment discourse of modernity up until the present day in the works of Habermas or Apel can be read as modifying the notion of an information community from a community of facts to a community of consensus. The notion of communicative consensus is a very appealing model for community in a modernist culture, for it elicits the clarity of language, which is assumed in the physical sciences, as well as evoking the scientific/philosophical ideal of solving a 'problem.' The problem, here, as in all liberal democratic political models, is the arrival of community so that the political whole reflects the will of the particular subjects (this is, however, the very same political aesthetics of mimesis which Walter Benjamin notes in the case of fascism in his essay, "The Work of Art in the Age of Mechanical Reproduction"). In such models of the state, the term 'public' refers to a total presence of 'the people' by means of their self-representation. Once again, language remains the problem for the imminent arrival of Reason in the community. In the communicational community of the democratic state each voice 'expresses' its views and tolerates the other view until a consensus is reached. What is missing from this discourse, however, are multiple dynamics of language: from issues involving the organization and judgment of what constitutes a valid 'view' or voice to ontological and psychological problems involving the 'self' understood as an indivisible individual capable of self-representation. What communicative communities require, despite themselves, is a return to a neo-Aristotelian notion of *polis,* though the regulative ideals for a community are no longer 'truths,' but rather, conditions for truth in rhetorical norms of communication.

This thoroughly *modernist* notion of a global 'virtual' site for the free play of ideas replicates what was, for Goethe, the site of *Weltliteratur.* As Antoine Berman argues, Goethe's notion of a world "market place" of ideas was intrinsic in defining German *Bildung* and nationalism as the formal site and model for such a 'world.'[11] Within our own day, this "*Spieltrieb*" is formed and destined by the figure of the 'United States' which appropriates the language(s) of English, the politics of democracy, the multiplicities of world trade, and the space of commerce to its own national character. The United States' picture of itself as an intrinsically multicultural nation becomes both the model and the destination for global internationalism through the form of 'information.' Such a picture of a controlled and rational *Weltsprache* is exactly the same as that of Goethe's *Weltliteratur,* founded upon a privileged, non-problematic, and appropriative mode of translation. As Berman points out in regard to Goethe (57), the metaphor of such national(ist) internationalism of ideas is that of the ideal capitalist marketplace, which in reality has never existed. But it is now through the standardization of information technology that national internationalism is allowed to continue its rhetoric of 'democracy,' 'international language,' 'world market,' and the 'global marketplace/village/community,' as if these terms referred to actual empirical objects and as if these terms were linked to a single national producer of technological and cultural goods. On a global scale, however, the term "information technology" is inadequate for assuring either the presence of voice or a community of meaning. "Information technology" can refer to the electronic and mechanical means that allow the transmission of some sort of semiotic mark. In the rhetoric of electronic democracy and the global virtual community, however, information technology not only explicitly connotes electronic technology, but implicitly, the techne of speech as self-representation. (Such a metaphorical transfer of the term from an electronic register to a social register seems analogous to the transfer of the word 'information' from Shannon's use of the term to its current synonymous relation with what might be signified by the terms 'representational communication.')[12] Simply put, there is no way that one can move from "information technology" to "information democracy" without reading "technology" in terms of "democracy"—that is, without reading the techne of information in terms of not only electronic transfer, but also, *political transfer*.

Such transfers encounter all the traditional problems of translation, including that of the appropriation of the other according to the origin's own self-image. The 'information community,' however, assumes a common discursive form as the backbone for its community. In the so-called 'post-Cold War' period, the common discourse is premised as capitalism, foremost the capitalism of the information age (that is, a transnational capital of information, and conversely, a capital of transnational information). But to say that global information will occur by capitalization, and at the same time, that capitalization is global information, is to set up a tautology of capital and information under the heading of the 'transnational.' Such a tautology begs the question of what type of semantic currency forms the economy of the transnational, and where such capital originates and comes due. It is often the reply of advocates of electronic democracy and virtual community that the answer to this question is, 'nowhere,' and such a reply is often accompanied by pointing to the non-topology (or better, trans-topology) of electronic networks. This reply, grounded in technology however, once again forgets that 'information' is now more than simply data exchange but connotes qualitative and quantitative judgments as to the meaning and form of information as a linguistic concern, and that the capitalization of this process in a transcultural manner is extremely problematic.

But to be skeptical for a moment, let us assume that this reply to the formation of capital is not a forgetting, but rather, a truth more truthful than we want to see. That, perhaps, pointing to the electronic machinery as the site of capital refers not to information capital, but to financial capital—to a type of capital that can, indeed, be measured qualitatively and quantitatively on a world market of financial goods. In this case, post-war capitalism constitutes the capitalization of information on a global scale, and the discourse of global information then assumes the capitalization of discourse through economic capitalization. Capitalism would then be the transnational language, par excellence, of information flow; it would be the reduction of language to the concerns of capitalism and capitalization. Thus, the problem of global information can be understood in terms of the Cold War task of bringing post-colonial (and post-communist) economies under a 'new world order' of global capitalization. "Capitalism" means here not only a financial economy, but the global reduction or centralization of language to this economy in order to fulfill the conditions for democratic representation in Western capitalist states—namely, a common rhetoric. This reduction or standardization of culture and language into a single global market can be accomplished in either industrial or postindustrial economies. Information technology, however, must be present in each country or region in order for transnational capitalism to flow in the form of information. Once again, however, what is of concern for both the 'new world' order of capitalism and of information is the *capitalization* of information. This capitalization is necessary to fulfil the conditions for a dreamed seamless flow of global information and the growth of such information in a regulated market. The "capitalization of information" means not only achieving the flow of information on a global surface of capitalism, but the promoting and privileging of 'information' in order to achieve that surface.

The privileging of certain rhetorical forms over others on a global scale means the imperialism of formal law over a universe of human speakers. Given the varieties of practices that could be called capitalistic, the further capitalization of language by capitalism is not an easily accomplished task. Postindustrial capitalism, however, is not national or even regional capitalism, but is transnational. The capital of postindustrial capitalism lies not in an electronic a-topos, but in a standardization of receptive and productive sites in national and regional centers. Such centers answer to the call of standardization by standardizing themselves in response to a dominant power and language. Such response of minor languages to a 'major' language is unheard of on a global scale. It is unheard of because, previously, living major languages were constituted by the minor language speakers who spoke them. As Deleuze and Guattari argue in the fourth chapter of *A Thousand Plateaus*, to be a major language means to be spoken according to minor languages—including pidgin forms of the language, and dialectical schisms.

The language of transnational capitalism, or what desires to be a global measure of capital, more resembles an idealized Latin, as it represents a class of ideological, financial, and political power masquerading under the banner of the '(common) good.' This language of transnational capitalism argues the rhetoric of information according to the rule of the spectacle. This rule, as stated by Giorgio Agamben is: "What appears is good; what is good appears" (80). The dissemination of speech and its constitution as meaning in the ear of the other should relatively increase as those ears expand, but instead, the larger the number of ears, the more the Same returns, and the less any true dialogue occurs. Such a rule severely restricts sensibility—in terms of what is physically acknowledgeable and what is cognitively judged—because what appears as usable information in transnational capitalism is that which is meaningful in terms of the producers of such information. Such circularity of production and judgment defines a national politics that is no longer national, but which now responds to the call of transnational capitalism, a call which is seen to be the only *possible one* for a global community. Global Being is read in terms of a communication of salvation, and *a salvation through standardized communication*. The salvation which is promised is not merely one of economic riches, but one of ecological and social harmony, and one of personal liberation. Such personal liberation is rooted in a bourgeois sense of self—where the self best expresses itself in a voice of the self rooted in opinion, inseparable from everyone and no one. The language of alienation is adequately explored in Marx's notion of the commodity and in Heidegger's notion of the "everyday" and thus needs no addition here. Giorgio Agamben, however, by re-reading Guy Debord's notion of the "spectacle" advances the notion of linguistic alienation from a modernist effect *of* ideological constructions of community to a postmodern standard *as* community. In this difference lies the very essence of information as it is commonly understood as a neutral and universal term and here lies its difference from a culturally fragmented notion of knowledge. Namely, we are no longer concerned with the "spectacle" as a *product* of the State or culture, but we now strive toward achieving a global *Bildung through* the spectacle:

> Whereas under the old regime the estrangement of the communicative essence of humans took the form of a presupposition that served as a common foundation, in the society of spectacle it is this very communicativity, this generic essence itself (i.e., language) that is separated in an autonomous sphere. What hampers communication is communicability itself; humans are separated by what unites them. Journalists and mediacrats are the new priests of this alienation from human linguistic nature... Even more than economic necessity and technological development, what drives the nations of the earth toward a single common destiny is the alienation from

linguistic being, the uprooting of all peoples from their vital dwelling in language. (82)

Such globalization of politics through language aims toward the aestheticization of politics and language by the containment of politics and language within the form of 'communication' and communicativity. As Agamben argues, such alienation of language from human beings (an alienation which penetrates to the level of personal relations, which by their very nature are not universal) also opens up the problem of language in the same way as transnationalism opens up the problems of national identity by extending the scale of formal identification to sublime lengths (65). The problem that is opened in each case is the problem of language's relation to a singular being and to a community of beings, and with that, the problem of singular being and community to identity. According to Agamben, the coming struggle will not be in regard to the type of state we desire, but will be a struggle between the state and the state-without-identity as the Being of community. As Agamben argues,

> The State can recognize any claim for identity—even that of a State identity within the State. What the State cannot tolerate in any way, however, is that the singularities form a community without affirming an identity, that humans co-belong without any representable condition of belonging (even in the form of a simple presupposition). The State, as Alain Badiou has shown, is not founded on a social bond, of which it would be the expression, but rather on the dissolution, the unbinding it prohibits. For the State, therefore, what is important is never the singularity as such, but only its inclusion in some identity, whatever identity (but the possibility of the whatever itself being taken up without an identity is a threat the State cannot come to terms with).... Whatever singularity, which wants to appropriate belonging itself, its own being-in-language, and thus rejects all identity and every condition of belonging, is the principal enemy of the State. (86-87)

What is implicitly argued here as a coming politics is not anarchy, because government is never mentioned. Government is no longer mentioned because government has given itself over to the State and in so doing has turned away from community in order to define that community as separate from itself (as governed *by it*, governed by that which *embodies* the law (and thus is that which is, or is largely above *the blows of the law*)). This may, however, be saying no more than that the relation of State and community has not essentially changed since the feudal kingdoms, and that the collapse of the rhetoric of representational democracy in the West—through economic abandonment by the oligarchy, through an appropriation and alienation of language by capital, and through the collapse of metaphysical assurances about the good of the (*or any*) "state"—has shown an historical contingency which the rhetoric of humanism vehemently denies.

The collapse of the rhetoric of "democracy" in the West lies in its inability to separate itself from major elements of fascism: namely, their common aestheticization of politics in the body of the State, their politicization of the arts by the active promotion of realism and the marginalization of questions of framing and form, and by their reduction of the total community to an imminent and uncomplicated 'common good' of 'good sense,' 'reality,' and reason. For Hegel, the difference between monarchy and democracy was a matter of linguistic technique: the *representation* of the people (*das Volk*) *as* the state and the *representation* of the state (*das Reich*) *as* the people. The problem in democracy was the Machiavellian control of language toward the spectacle of the organic nation. As Heidegger's complex involvement in politics, as well as his repeated protests against the alienating effects of modernism in *Being and Time* and his earlier lecture at the Marburg Theological Society (published in English as *The Concept of Time*) show, what Nancy calls the "abandonment of Being" develops out of, and in opposition to, modernist problematics which are not reducible to the history of philosophy, though they share philosophical forms.[13]

Post-apocalypse, Anti-salvation, or the Way Things are Down Here

The language of global liberation through global information constitutes a contemporary rhetoric for an immanent community, and it promises the renewal of humanism's claims to knowledge (which currently buckle under social fact in the West). Against this model of community, as immanently to-come, we may analyze the community that *is*, a community that comes after "divine abandon" and therefore after the utopian claims of modernist politics. Such a postmodern sense of community is post-apocalyptical in the sense of an unrecoverable failure and abandonment of cultural containment by political utopias; it is a tallness from nothing into nothing. Implicit with such an understanding of community would be an understanding of *logos* as that which does not constitute a separate sphere from human being, nor as that which is simply constituted by the speech of an individual, but instead, is that which neither imminent nor immanent but is somehow related to that which is. "What is" is called by Agamben, "whatever," and it is spoken of in terms of "singularity" (rather than as indivisible individuality). Such singularity is neither a formal essence nor an individual existence, and thus it cannot dialectically bring formal essence into being by individual existence (such apocalyptical essences may be read in terms of Reason or in terms of 'clear and distinct' meaning or in terms of the "true" State). Such singularity, by denying identity as either essence or existence, lies in the utter bankruptcy of dialectics.

As some have suggested, in Heidegger's *Being and Time* the thinking of *Mitsein* (being-with) is suppressed by thinking *Dasein* (the existence of man) in terms of its lone relation to death. But such a suggestion is unfounded, because for Heidegger the experience of death is an experience only gotten from another. So too, in Jean-Luc Nancy's *The Inoperable Community* and Maurice Blanchot's *The Negative Community*, love marks a tracing and retracing of one's common essential finitude in a relation with another. Love and death operate, here, as traces of a relation to, the impossible. Both writers, working out of a tradition of Heidegger's "The Origin of the Work of Art" and the works of Derrida, think art in terms of a drawing out of these traces. The face to face with the impossible is not an encounter with an immanence to come, but with what is. Heidegger marks this moment of encounter as a moment of anxiety, when Being retreats and beings as a whole press near.

The everyday world falls away for *Dasein* and the nothing (*das Nicht*) of every(thing) presses close. Language, in its stuttering gesture attempts to think this exposure of *Dasein* to the nothing. This is the moment which Heidegger marks in terms of art and the beginnings of science (as a response to the question of the reality of the world—a question which links all the sciences together, historically, and epistemologically, in the name, and even the method, of Western philosophy). (It is because each science departs from this original question, in the mode of thesis and method (that is, in the mode of a uniquely destined reply that can be thought in terms of metaphor—"as" (Heidegger, Gasché, Agamben, Derrida)), that the world cannot be explained by any one science, nor the experience of the world by science itself.)

Thus, 'communication' and system originate in a thinking of the impossible. Such an originating communication is a response to the call of Being—that is, what is—in its original strangeness of difference. Each response to the call is specific to the speaker, and yet general as each speaker is bound by the call of the question—the call of finitude. Such an original communication constitutes the community of speakers, and it presupposes what we today think in terms of 'communicative communities' in the mode of identities and the correspondence of meaning between 'individuals.' The freedom of free inquiry that mark such liberal communities and the sciences must, as Chris Fynsk suggests (Nancy, *The Inoperative Community*, xi ff.), be thought as an *event* rather than as a given of this or that political system. It is that event wherein the world is given in terms that *demand* a reply. Such a reply, as Blanchot notes, is singular and not reducible to rumor or opinion ("The Most Profound Question," 19-20). *It cannot be stressed too heavily that a reply is not simply an answer. A reply is a response to a call that demands a reply by sharing in the alterity of its answer. Conversely, the demand of a reply is always already contained within its answer. Reply is, thus, an ethical demand, and it is not just any answer that is being called for. Reply is part of a relay whose origin cannot be addressed other than in the repetition of the reply, and thus, whose destination cannot be immediately determined.* Reply, however, is not agreement nor disagreement, but rather stands prior to all systematics in acknowledging the seriousness with which it must answer. In the seriousness of the reply, alterity is acknowledged, and though the meaning of the reply may be understood by others in-jest, the reply's gesture is not consumable but remains in the long-standing priority of the call and the consuming alterity which marks it.

(It may be added that there exist calls which ask for a reply, but which may only deserve an answer (and this "deserve" does not at all mean something derogatory, indeed an answer can be quite helpful). The demand of a call for a reply does not lie in individual intention, but in the im-possibility of fulfilling it—in reference to what, as Derrida argues, Benjamin refers to as "pure language" (*reine Sprache*). In other words, it is a question to which we *must* reply, even though we know of our mutual inadequacy.)

The ethical demand of a reply is tied to its positioning of the replier in terms of freedom. There is nothing 'good' or 'bad' in giving an answer—there is no ethical demand here (though there may be 'good' or 'bad' social consequences to the answerer for a specific answer—and these may be quite severe and may indeed lead back to an ethical demand. Thus, for example in the case of a prisoner being tortured for information, an answer may very quickly give way to a reply, and a reply provide an answer to the torturer's inquiry).

It is imperative to note also, however, given the political age we live in—an age of the erasure of history by the spectacular rule of alienated representation—that is, the repetition of the Same—that the reply, as repetition, is not a repeating of the Same in a new temporality. To constitute a relay of reply, each reply must acknowledge trauma, not in terms of the law of the Same, but in terms of alterity. The reply of Babel says both God's proper name and God's representations in multiple languages whose inadequacies lie not in the languages themselves, but in the alterity of Benjamin's "pure language." We must be careful not to assert the priority of representations over the original trauma in such a way as to forget the relation of the original trauma to law. The trauma, or origin, is such that each reply must acknowledge the origin's *alterity to itself.* In the political unconscious, as the personal unconscious, the representations do not tell the whole story of the trauma, nor constitute the trauma, and to think that they do invites the erasure of history. "History" in this sense is not to be thought of in terms of the representations of 'history,' but, in terms of the resistance to the repetition of the Same across time. The repeated blows of the law bring the law into being, but they cannot constitute the law any more than the child's repetitions can constitute the father. The law as Law—that is, as repetitions of the Same—is constituted by the form of the State. The State gives form to the polis (—in fact, is the form of the political today—), as well as the unconscious, as Law, as the repetition of the Same. In all translation, the Law of representation must be made explicit. In terms of community, we are speaking of the end of the dialectic between State and individual by the breaking of the form of the State, that is, the ideal silence of translation.

As the being-called by finitude (*Dasein*), the repliers are bound together (*Mitsein*) in a manner that eventually gives way to specialized responses and specialized identities in the manner of Western rhetoric. Death is exemplary among all the exposures of human being to the world, however, in that it cannot be worked upon methodologically (Nancy, *The Inoperative Community*, 15)—there is no science and can be no science which takes death per se as its object. Love, too, is exemplary in that its activities trace and retrace a difference between two people that both binds them and gives them singularity.

Love is, in this sense, the subtle marking and remarking of finitude which death makes loudly explicit.

As Nancy writes, "finitude always presents itself in being-in-common" (28). Quite expectedly, death can only be at first seen through the death of another. Only the experience of community can give us our death and our birth, through the death and birth of another (26). The communication of death is not a communication that is a transference of meaning, since death is quickly exhausted of meaning. For Heidegger in *Being and Time*, what is heard in death is a response to our own being-toward-death which binds us as human beings. In both death and love, one is ek-statically drawn out of the everyday world, and returned to a mode of being beyond one's self—not in the sense of being everyone and no one, but in the sense of being specifically one's self, as a singularity without essence, but full of reply. Such ek-stasis is not a communion of seamless union, but is a reunion to the seams which bind human beings as a community of singularities.

Liberal democratic thought which structures the thinking of information today requires that thinking be rational according to a certain ratio or measure determined by metaphysical thought and political hearsay. Individual and community commune according to that ratio. Within the tradition, singularity is thought by the correspondence between what is and what is to come, according to categories of propriety and appropriation—according to individuality. The measure for propriety is found in Being, God, or scientific law (for us, economic capitalism) in the tradition which Heidegger calls "ontotheological." Thus, for such thought, a human being is "true" and "good" only as he or she represents him or her self in that mode of reason, that is, according to a measure which determines the mode of beings-as-a-whole, as well as individually. Human beings are said to give themselves the ability to be recognized as human beings by God, by themselves, and by other human beings according to rules of decency, truth, and taste. But here, temporal conditions for such recognition remain unthought, and what is worse, what is truly immanent—that is, what is common—is deleted. Namely, that re-cognition, as well as cognition, always already acknowledge that which allows such dialectics to exist—namely a difference that is common. One is not human because of this or that specific quality which one gives to oneself in terms of representation or is given to one by some other human being, but rather, one is human as far as what commonly joins human beings (namely, a relation to finitude and language). "Human rights" are not a condition of this or that technology of speech (this or that electronic machinery, or this or that group or identity), nor are human rights given by this or that state, but instead, they are inherent in the gesture of reply to the limit itself (that is, to the gesture of the human animal). As such, human rights (that is, the right of humanness) cannot be granted by the state, though the state can displace this *given* of human beings onto a standard language or rhetoric. Language is shared and plural, and it is given by the im-possible, which is both transcendental and explicit in the translational reply.

This sharing of language constitutes the announcement of alterity in language. Within the horizon of time, this announcement is infinitely finite, and brings into appearance the historicity of the speakers. In his book on Plato's "*hermeneia*," *Sharing Voices*, Nancy writes:

> The sharing (the dialogue) is understood here as a provisional necessity, whether this is fortunate or unfortunate, whether it is an enrichment or an impediment to the community of interlocutors...It is made of and by the sharing: it understands the sharing to be infinitely finished (completed) in the other by the other, in you by me, in us by us. And it is comprehended by the sharing. The community remains to think according to the sharing of the *logos*. (247)

If we are to rethink "communication" in terms of the announcement of the other—that is, as community, we must rethink information as something other than the inclusion of the subject within in-formed systems of thought. Since the call which elicits community is primarily that of finitude, it is a singularly uncanny (*unheimlich*), and indeterminate call. The determining of indetermination occurs through a process of informing where *such* is determined *as such* and *such* a thing. We have earlier alluded to the role played by metaphor in the sciences, and analogously, we may now think the appearance of beings *as such* in terms of their informing.[14]

Communication, as the community of *logos*, is not only a sharing of *logos*, but the contact of singularities with surfaces or forms of meaning, including systems of identities. Though no communication within such informational surfaces can exhaust or define the community, nor define the pure exteriority of such surfaces (no matter how rigidly borders are defined from within, borders are defined by exclusion, and thus incorporate the other within their metalanguage), their formal characteristics are part of the 'between' from which the in-forming of information proceeds. Singularities are not exhausted by identity, but on the other hand, they are not existential individuals: they trace out by their exposures at their limit. By means of these singular variations, identity is marked in terms of difference. Identity, as such, is thus never identical to itself but continually virtual.

In the same way, the "virtual community" is that community that can never be other than how it is, as non-identical to itself. As such, all communities are virtual, not due to their potential fulfillment, nor due to their representative a-topos, but by virtue of their always temporal being. (The virtuality of community was always present within the apocalyptical tradition but the virtual was always promised as a temporary condition, as a means or form to an end; indeed, the condition of time in its coming to itself through history). There is no such thing as identity or nonidentity, rather, traces of a person in their listening to the other. The others, in their otherness, are at the limit, and such a limit is the limit of surfaces, a limit that allows a double meaning to the notion of "exposure" in regard to singularities (see endnote above). Agamben refers to this variation as "usage" or "ethos" (20). Ethics cannot be exhausted because the practice of listening at the limit to the call of the other (a call that is shared in finitude) is highly temporal and specific. Ethical Being is the event of freedom that depends on listening and on the tracing of reply into a world. As reply, it too depends on a listening and on a reply. Such bonding of each through each is the source for meaning: even when we talk to ourselves we have meaning only through an internalized other. This sharing of language is what Nancy means by "dialogue."

If to speak is to be called to reply, and if to "mean" is to be similarly listened to and replied to, then we cannot reduce speech and meaning to an ex-pression of one's self, nor to a talk wherein both speech and reply are both everyone's and no one's. Similarly, "speech" as a call to us to speak need not be limited to human beings, nor "meaning" to a reply of only a certain type of being in relation to finitude (namely, for Heidegger, *Dasein*). Finitude need not be experienced in the mode of *Dasein* in order to appear. In our relations with 'animals,' for example, finitude is always present, not through the experience of death or freedom, but in the manner of love, through a marking and remarking of an always already joining that can never come under the illusion of universal understanding. The community of the animal—a community which the human is always part of and never separate from, even within an ontologically inscribed specificity—is in fact the event, par excellence, for the experience of the otherness of the other, and for the experience of one's own finitude on a universal scale. In our relations with 'the animal,' the commonality of the limits and joining of language is a commonality whose extension along lines of the body is quite explicit. This is the commonality and the dissemination of Spinoza's "extension," a thinker and a term utilized by Agamben to think commonality and by Deleuze and Guattari to think their concept of the Body Without Organs. It will behoove us, in the next chapter, to think through the in-(>)forming of community which is proper to the body on a universal scale, one animal to the next, without clear delineation; that is, while maintaining singularities, including that of *Dasein* in its exposure.

"If we could talk to the animals... ":: De-creation

The Limits of "Man"

> Community means, consequently, that there is no singular being without another singular being, and that there is, therefore, what might be called, in a rather inappropriate idiom, an originary or ontological "sociality" that in its principle extends far beyond the simple theme of man as a social being (the *zoon politikon*, the political animal, is secondary to this community). For, on the one hand, it is not obvious that the community of singularities is limited to "man" and excludes, for example, the "animal" (even in the case of "man" it is not *a fortiori* certain that this community concerns only "man" and not also the "inhuman" or the "superman," or, of course, "woman": after all, the difference between the sexes is itself a singularity in the difference of singularities). On the other hand, if social being is always posited as a predicate of man, community would signify on the contrary the basis for thinking only something like "man." But this thinking would at the same time remain dependent upon a principal determination of community, namely, that there is no communion of singularities in a totality superior to them and immanent to their common being.

> (Nancy, *The Inoperative Community*, 28)

Traditionally in the Western cultural tradition, beginning with Aristotle's exclusion of human beings from animals by the criteria of the *logos*, so-called 'animals' constitute the negative background upon which the figure of 'man' is constituted. Thus, as Derrida finely argues, even in Heidegger's work, the work of language is understood as the tracing and retracing this figure of man, and within this figure, spirit can be authenticated in terms of a further working of language proper to man, namely, history.[15]

The border between man and animal is the most closely guarded border of reason, especially in terms of language. The secret to language's closeness to man, namely its rationality, however, is breached by Heidegger's destruction of the ontotheological tradition, and with it the rational origins for the technological "world view." Language regains its deeply human space for Heidegger, however, in its relation to the question of Being. In the question of Being (experienced as an opening, breach, or caesura (in the experience of being-toward-death or in Heidegger's later writings in historical breaches)), poetic language traces the relation between human existence (*Dasein*) and the nothing (*das Nicht*) before it. As has been noted by others, such as Christopher Fynsk, Heidegger's co-primordial term for the event of truth in *Being and Time*, namely, *Mitsein* or beingwith, is not as fully developed as being-toward-death and anxiety in that work. It is my contention that what is at stake in the forgetting of *Mitsein* is not only (as Jean-Luc Nancy has suggested in *The Inoperative Community*) the avoidance of the *communal nature* of the experience of death (as an experience only understood through another's death), but even more determinately, such an individual analytic avoids the very serious ruptures that occur along the border of humans and 'animals.'

I think that it must be recognized that even with the thinking that takes Heidegger's thought the furthest, this thought largely confines itself within the philosophical proper, that is within the thinking of human understanding and finitude. For this claim, I would point to the reading of "mood" (*Stimmung*) in terms of voice or style. What is forgotten is the indetermination of mood, and yet its responsiveness. This indetermination leaves the borders of individual *Dasein* open, not only to other human existences, but to other modes of Being. Properly speaking, it leaves open the destruction of ontology as metaphysics. Whether such an inquiry is truly specific to man, however, is open to doubt, in the sense that it cannot be said to be either a true or false assertion once human response can no longer be said to be the sole reply to the call of Being. That is to say, once language can no longer be said to be rational, or be a response to human experiences of finitude, the specificity of language to "man" is lost, as well as its carefully erected and patrolled border. One of the paradoxes involving language and animals which is passed on from Aristotle involves dreams. According to Aristotle, animals, lacking language, do not dream. But this seems contrary to, at least, a cursory observation of our pets. Steering aside the question of the *content* of the unconscious, however, there is the problem of the *formation* of the unconscious. For Freud, this formation is a result of a social impact—namely the threat of castration in the language and law of the father. Through primary repression this impact is forgotten, but repeated, and in fact, inscribed (according to Derrida) by empirical repetitions.[16]

But no one who has ever had a pet with them is unfamiliar with this disciplinary 'training.' Nor is any pet owner surprised that the very repetition of a gesture both strengthens the 'law of the father' as well as marks (at least for the owner) the boundary which joins the two (or more) species. In fact, the negotiation often enjoined to the law speaks of a variability in the inscription as well as its appearance as Law, and there is every indication in dealing with a 'difficult' animal that the boundary between the two species is fluid for both, and thus that the law is neither singular nor absolute. There are even times when it seems that the other species takes delight in playing with the human limitation, and in this case, introduces a strong sense of variability into the relation. One of my two cats, for example, will tease me at night, coming toward the door and then running off, with a seeming knowledge of my inability to see her at night (contrary to her own ability to see me). She will come home, but in this case, she clearly determines the enactment of law. That pet cats, for example, need to accommodate themselves to us, as we to them, indicates a fluidity to being-with that is evident in a language that joins the two species together in a common mode of living. That within species there are also acts of language marking singularities to Being is evident in the incredible jealousy one cat will show the other when the other is getting attention. This is language, not simply as communication, but more primordially as gesture of reply. It is language not at the limits of a given being in relation to itself (for *Dasein*, its relation to the human experience of death), but at the limits of its own speciesness. No more radical gesture for language can be thought than between species, but the gesture of reply is less constituted by the failure of understanding before an abyss than it is by the fluid passing of the other in and out of our daily life, thus encasing that daily life in care (*Sorge*). An ethos of listening, otherness, translation and sharing of language and community is more available by thinking the human animal/not-human animal bond than by appealing to a sense of community poisoned by the idealism of utopian humanism. The community is a community of beingwith as animals, and the mode in which finitude is shared is that of patience and time. Though a high degree of *calculative* time may be particular to humans in larger groups (though non-calculative *futurity* seems much better developed in migrating birds and in squirrels preparing for winter, etc.), time is certainly *created* by patience between, at least, domesticated animals (I include humans in this bonding). The cat sits patiently as I type on the computer, waiting for me to give her attention. The patient enactment of time other animals show in regard to human beings far exceeds what humans show in relations with one another in and especially what they show other beings. "Man" is, indeed, the forgetting animal. While Enlightenment ideals may trace universal ideals upon singular relationships, animals inscribe a temporality that, though less calculative, is no less far ranging, both in terms of time and in terms of scope of consideration or care. For in the relation of moods (including the moods or modes of species in relation to 'one another') temporality is marked by increments of gestures of reply that are *sensed* rather than 'known.' Nietzsche's appeal to senses other than cognitive sight (especially smell), his emphasis upon the body (see the first book of *Zarathustra*), and Zarathustra's company of animals (and, in addition, Nietzsche's description of the modern political state as *"Untier"*—literally, the negation of the animal, or more animal than animal) here join the animal's sense of smell and its *senses* of foreboding, friendliness, and time. It is the *delicateness* and *carefulness* of these senses that is *Mitsein*.

If information is to be thought as the representation of data or as a pragmatics of information flow or even as the communication of finitude, we must confront the problem of thinking information-language in relation to a metaphysical anthropomorphism—humanism—and confront the question of the animal. It is only through confronting the 'vagaries' of the animal that the immanent community of 'man' can be adequately critiqued, understanding circumscribed, and information displaced from its metaphysical inscriptions.

Certainly, as has been suggested throughout this paper, the model of information as representation is dubious on many fronts, foremost that it composes itself around a notion of a universal material immanence that is most properly understood in the mind of man. As Derrida has suggested, such an understanding of matter, as evidence speaking for itself to man, is most firmly grounded in the trope of (human) "speech" as auto-affective, and as the true expression of a fully rational individual.

Thus, the curious twist to Wittgenstein's aphorism, "If a lion could talk, we could not understand him" (*Philosophical Investigations*, 223e). Wittgenstein is here speaking of the strange, uncanny, or perhaps we can even say, *unheimlich* experience of entering a "foreign country" (223e) (a metaphor for the "enigma" of the other) and he is arguing that though we may know the language of the country we still may not know their way of life (and thus, we will not understand the meaning of their words). Understanding here, as earlier in the *Investigations*, is not a question of finding the 'true' meaning of words, but rather, of being able to perform acts that are said to be true by the other. Information is, here, that which is useful outside of strict limitations of correspondence (and thus, no absolute criteria could be achieved for what is useful or not, relevant or not). Like the conditional statement regarding animal speech in *Dr. Doolittle* ("If we could talk to the animals..."), the possibility of animal speech is seen as something at the edge of language (or at least the metaphysics of language). Despite Wittgenstein's own predilection toward a pragmatics of language, both speech and a certain human understanding (separate from a lion's "understanding") are patrolled by this conditional "if" along the border of human propriety. (Therefore, all the behaviorists absurdities of humans teaching apes 'language,' etc..) The fact is that we are always already talking to the animals and they to us by virtue of our being-with 'them' in this world. That we share a world with other animals gives us the very ability to be 'not-them.' And it is in this sharing and continual coming into a world that the notion of a singularly human world may emerge. The question is not whether we are 'talking' to animals, and they are talking to us (this talk becomes more and more indistinguishable the more domestic we become with one another, as happens with persons, also), but rather, what is the nature of that communication of *Mitsein*, and what is said (i.e., what is information there?)

Because for Wittgenstein, speech is bound to species categories, communication becomes trivialized along the borders of human understanding. Wittgenstein's rejection of psychologism prevents him from thematizing these conditions of the understanding in a non-pragmatic way ("They [psychological conditions] are not readily accessible" he states immediately above the lion statement). But by the same pragmatic reasoning, the understanding of the lion, too, cannot be readily separated from that of the human. Contrary to Wittgenstein's notion of entering "into a strange country with entirely strange traditions," it is the very strangeness of *every* speech act that requires a pragmatic territorialization of meaning. As Nancy remarks in his analysis of the Platonic *hermeneia*, and I believe it is a central point in Derrida's critique of Searle and Austin's theory of speech acts, it is the uncanniness or indeterminateness of every speech act which requires the criteria of pragmatic meaning. In other words, language gains meaning only by being shared, in the sense that it becomes meaningful only because of this sharing. As Nancy argues, such sharing is prior to interpretation, and is grounded in the gesture of reply. When it comes to talking with animals, we must take Nancy's argument further, and deconstruct the privilege of 'rational' responses over others as the grounds for community. Such a deconstruction of the privileging of 'rational' enunciation would follow that of the destruction of the purely *human* community as the community where speech and understanding are the same (the community of *logos*), and where *logos* defines the purely human community. The danger lies not only in defining a human community, but in blocking other traits of the human which make humans part of an animal community (and thus, *give* human specificity by means of a temporal working out of difference). It is by means of such blockage that human specificity enters the anthropomorphism of humanism. Questions coming to a 'reasonable' resolution do mark humans as humans, but the conversation of their animality, that is, their common difference, is marked whether their 'view' is agreed upon or not. No agreement is such that it is certain now and forever. When we talk with one another, agreement forms a very minute element of what we do—mostly we reply. This is true of human interaction with even the most exact information systems.

The "subject" field within a bibliographical database can be used for years, even by professional academics, without being sure of 'what it means' or how exactly it is to be used. Nor, as the Habermasians might suggest, is it true that we must have rational understanding to have understandable meaning. A correspondence response within a mechanical system is a very simple model of reply because the range of use and counterreply is limited to the *fulfillment* of a task. Our interactions with animals, however, are not so different than with each other. That is to say, our interactions with animals preserve what is essential to our relations with one another: namely, the finite infinity of conversations with the 'other,' and the innateness of such conversations in any meaning. The relay of reply comes before any meaning can be arrived at. *Meaning is not a destination inherent within language by means of either rhetoric, 'ordinary language' or hidden language games (i.e., 'contexts'), but is a pragmatic stabilization of assemblages of expectations between a listener and a listener (this statement applies to self-address as well, though often this fact is overlooked). Language speaks as a relay of replies which precede any speaker, 'context,' or meaning. Language lies 'before' them, and because of this, the community of 'us' lies before any 'one.'* After Derrida's critique of Lacan, we may say that there is no reason the letter must reach its destination, because there is no destination for a letter to reach outside of its reception. *Simply, there is no more reason to limit such dialogue of reply to any one 'species' of animal (i.e., 'man'), than there is to limit such reply to 'men,' 'rational persons,' 'normal persons,' 'well-educated persons,' 'science,' etc...* In fact, such terms designate idealized locations of repression that constitute nothing and no one, because they assume what 'all know' (all the ones who 'count') is true and absolutely well-known.[17] The idealized location of Absolute Being (Science, or *Wissenschaft*) is in this sense the mass knowledge of *Alltäglichkeit*. The idealized Hegelian state of the *Volk* is, thus, both absolutely vulgar and absolutely idealized, that is, it is the embodiment, as in the case of the popular culture of National Socialism, of the fascist state.[18] *Humanism, in its attribution of reply from and only to the human, is the fascism of the human. The random consumption, destruction, and the absolute negation of the liberal category of 'rights' to the 'animal' can say no more.* Within the philosophical tradition, humanism absolutely forbids the notion of 'inter-species' communication, community, or even more radically in Deleuze and Guattari's terms, 'becoming animal.' *There is, simply, no more important and transcendentally protected category than the human, and no more consumed and expelled category than the 'animal.' The question of the animal is, before all other questions, the question of 'man.'* It is no accident that the position of the not-man and the animal—the woman (as "plant" in Hegel), the (Black) 'races' (in Hume and Kant, as apes or missing links) are continually bound together: *The category of 'the animal' symbolizes the absolute territorialization and classification of humans across their own society. It is the first and last category which excludes the community, and which defines a community and thus the community.* 'The human' is the category of categories for humanism and science understood as law, and as such it constitutes the essence of rational 'humanity.'

In many ways, the question of community posed by Nancy is duplicated in the problem of the animal, except on a much larger, more primary scale. The question is not whether animals can talk with 'us 'or 'us' with 'them' (the ridiculousness of such semantics is evident if 'we' remember that 'we' *are* animals), but by what violence of metaphysics (particularly that of humanism) does this dualism become a problem, much less an impossibility? How is it that the human species becomes so distinct that that which joins community (the gesture of reply), that which is between species (both giving them their difference, as well as joining them), becomes the property of man? Or, to put this question in a slightly more Heideggerian framework, how does the gesture of reply become equivalent to human specificity itself? Is not the very question of *Dasein's* Being a question of *Dasein's* joining with other animals—a joining that is not simply marked with every gesture in terms of *Dasein's* Being, but a difference which, by virtue of being beyond *Dasein* exceeds the understanding and exceeds the techne of design and inscription which gives *Dasein* its specific Being. No matter how much "man" may mark this distinction, such inscription cannot give the sum of man's Being in the community of animals. If this were so, if human animals were simply "man" (as the Western tradition, including Heidegger, argue when arguing against 'the animal' in terms of *logos*), then all relations with animals in non-cognitive modes would have to be abandoned (and with it, the radical critique begun by Nietzsche upon humanism). In the face of the question of the animal, the retreat of Heideggerian thought back to the specificity of *Dasein* in terms of ontology attempts to 'save' the abandonment of human Being to its animalness. The analysis of *Dasein,* only in terms of its relation to its own specific question of Being in terms of *logos*, continues the human-centeredness of humanism and rolls against the de-creationism of Nietzsche's critique. *The animal must be thought in terms other than consumption, sacrifice, and a categorical exclusion* (by means of inclusion and ingestion) *of the animal. And this means, since humans too are animals, that human as well as non-human communities must be thought, always already in terms other than consumption, sacrifice, and categorical exclusion* (and this includes, lest I 'eat my words, which may be as tough as beef' and you 'just can't swallow it,' consumptive metaphors for the understanding).

"Becoming-Animal..."

Gilles Deleuze and Felix Guattari in *A Thousand Plateaus* (the second book in *Capitalism and Schizophrenia*) propose, particularly in their tenth chapter, "1730: Becoming-Intense, Becoming-Animal, Becoming-Imperceptible...," a radically universal manner of thinking the space of finitude between animals. Seemingly coming from a reading of Spinoza's *Ethics*, they postulate "lines" or "planes" according to shared expressions of organisms (planes of "consistency or composition," the most primary being that of "extension," which for Spinoza was one of the two attributes of God by which we can postulate his existence as infinity (i.e., all beings have extension)). Deleuze and Guattari seem to perform a positive reading of finitude, rather than the negative reading which comes out of a German tradition epitomized by Hegel's philosophy. It is a thinking of the same problems of alterity and finitude, but from the aspect of *the finitude of all beings in their joining*, rather than the joining of all beings in their finitude.

For Deleuze and Guattari, all beings are primarily becomings in that they are in constant contact vis-a-vis planes of consistency. Such planes are informational lines in the sense that they are not so much previously categorized or in-formed lines, as lines in-forming beings through extensional contact with other 'organisms.' Information, in this sense, is a given of finitude and being-in-theworld, rather than something developed by thought. "Thought" (the second of Spinoza's two attributes of God known to human beings) can be read, however, as constituting a vertical plane of 'organ-ization' and development in a species, and is what we usually think of as organizing an organism or a body according to the 'reason' or the essential Being of an organism. Information 'flows' in thought according to an idealized formal system that makes up the body of the animal as species-organism. In the Western tradition, thought is given overwhelming precedence over extension, and it is reified as a founding category for all that is via the mind of God. Subsequently, information is understood solely in terms of an idealized organic systematicity, rather than through asymmetrical and non-congruous contacts. The result is the hierarchization of nature according to a reification and closure of "thought." It is upon this vertical plane that the 'bodies' of the state, individual, and other social organisms are analogically identified and then metaphorized according to the Same.

Through their discussion of becoming and 'the animal,' Deleuze and Guattari force us not only to think what they call "the body without organs" (bodies composed according to the plane of consistency), but force us to reconsider "information" flows outside of systematicity. "Communication," they explain with reference to Bergson, is not the exchange of data among equal organisms which possess the same modes of understanding and duration, but of the interaction of heterogeneous beings who do indeed "coexist" with each other and make sense of each other in spite of different modes of Being (238). ("Coexistence" does not mean, of course, a Greek or Christian sense of immanent harmony since there is no ratio or *logos* by which such a community could be formed. Common extension is not imminent, but explicit.) As Deleuze and Guattari argue, contact does not occur by identification, nor does it lead to or produce any planned or teleological thing (239). Thus, information and communication cannot be limited to exchange, and the total constriction of such terms within the question of man, and most of all the question of the understanding, proves illegitimate.

The importance of thinking information other than in terms of identification and exchange or systemic "flow" not only applies to thinking the interaction of humans with other animals, but also in thinking the relation of humans and machines. For example, no mimetic model of the understanding can adequately explain lines of addiction that join humans and computers. The importance of Deleuze and Guattari's arguments lie in their ability to speak of information in modes other than that of the understanding, and to begin thinking *Mitsein* in terms of moods or zones of non-homogenous 'interpenetration' and monstrous becomings. The problem of the relation of desire and mood in the informing of organisms has hardly been explored.

Becomings occur in Deleuze and Guattari according to lines of proximity rather than by identification. Or perhaps we could add that identification can occur for certain beings due to the priority of proximity. Proximity constitutes a zone, or rather an inter-zone, that lies between two organisms. "Between two organisms" does not signify the priority of organisms and the between that happens to be between them, but rather, the between that lies before them according to planes of continuity and is that which they enter as one of their variations. Such deterritorializations of the organism of organization by lines of continuity are conditions always already there; they constitute the joining of beings according to planes such as extension and finitude, and constitute what Heidegger refers to as "the call of Being." The "inter-zones" of proximity constitute a radicality of this call that all beings reply to. Beings reply to this call in their interactions with one another, a reply that is formally universal and historically specific. This is what Spinoza means when he speaks in his *Ethics* of the infinity of substance, not according to number, but formally. "Infinity" is the name for the in-common of finite beings.

The "inter-zone" (we use this term, acknowledging not only Deleuze and Guattari's "zone," but also the work of William S. Burroughs) is a "site" of translations as far as it concerns a site where two zones are brought into a commonality that marks an originary "trait," trace, or seam of difference. The "interzone" is a zone where, as Deleuze and Guattari put it:

> [D]etteritorialization is always double, because it implies the coexistence of a major variable and a minor variable in simultaneous becoming (the two terms of a becoming do not exchange places, there is no identification between them, they are instead drawn into an asymmetrical block in which both change to the same extent, and which constitutes their zone of proximity). (306)

This is to say that the (inter)zone is a zone of defamiliarization, estrangement, and monstrosity. Within its certain uncertainty, size is released to relative indetermination, while specificity is maintained by a line of continuity which binds two orders at their limits. Thus, to use Deleuze and Guattari's example, the bird and the painting are married in color and line (304) (even art is not imitative, but the defamiliarization of both what the artist sees and what the bird 'is'—two modes of expression—in line and color); the cat is somewhat Oedipalized, but the "owner" is effaced as "man"—keeper and guardian of nature—by the refusal of the cat to be fully "my" pet. "I" touch a cat means that "cat" touches me. I get a viral infection means that the viral infection gets me. The sharing of qualities may be understood or not understood by an organism (as in the case of those animals for whom the ultraviolet spectrum is more evident than for us); it doesn't matter how we reply, but the fact that we do reply to a condition of sharing. We could extend this analysis to the point of seeing all interactions as "interzonal" and thus, stable zones as more or less regulating agencies of representation, what Deleuze and Guattari term vertical "planes of organization and development" which more provide categories for the understanding and for prescriptive practices of human development that they provide descriptions of the world. Thus, the chemical that "I" apply to my garden is not only changed by my application of it, but as I come into contact with it, physical changes result that may or may not be understood as significant upon 'my' body, depending on the threshold of measure and the categories of representation. Questions of human benefits or "effects" are secondary to zones of informing and the mutual informing that takes place and which cannot be reduced to a single, symmetrical result. *Information "flows" are first of all a-systemic* in that they cannot contain and limit mutations from contact. Procedures may be available for controlling these mutations into a system of inputs and outputs, however, and setting up an organized and developing zone (an "informed" zone): for example, a vaccine may slow or make ineffectual a virus within the human body, thus allowing it to circulate without a crippling effect upon the 'host.' But in general, relations between beings grow outward; they create mutations that may then be reterritorialized by agencies into information patterns. Overload is due to an increase in what may be considered "relevant," but this criterion is itself due to increased mutations along a certain line of continuity. Even within the sciences, where there are strict methodological and linguistic laws upon what is to be considered "relevant," information "grows" instead of becoming more simple ("simplicity"—this dream of philosophy and science—is clearly counterfactual to their own history).

Deleuze and Guattari stress that the "line" or "block" of the interzonal which passes between organisms gives them their singularity. What passes between organisms, that is to say what joins them along a plane of continuity, along a line of in-(>)forming, constitutes what Deleuze and Guattari call a "body without organs." This is a body that is constituted by its exteriority rather than by its interiority. Memory and identity are constituted by means of a history of contact, rather than by a reflective recovery of 'self' along an imaginary plane:

> From this point of view, one may contrast a childhood block, or a becoming-child, with the childhood memory: "a" molecular child is produced..."a" child coexists with us, in a zone of proximity or a block of becoming, on a line of deterritorialization that carries us both off—as opposed to the child we once were, whom we remember or fantasize, the molar child whose future is the adult. (294, ellipsis in original)

In the repetition or refrain of 'one,' a singularity deterritorializes its 'self' along a plane of continuity according to proximity (Deleuze and Guattari term this a "line of flight" and find it intrinsic to all becomings; Agamben too seems to express this thought in his thinking of "whatever" and the duality of "exposure.") Such deterritorialization is always already occurring, though it is, and may be repressively, controlled and reterritorialized by planes of development and organization. Throughout Deleuze and Guattari's work, "music" constitutes both a line of escape for voice, as well as signifies a trope for becoming. Particularly, it is "refrain" which is important, because by its original variability a theme is arrived at. As with translation, the trace of becoming-being is marked by a reply to an originary joining. The nature of the reply may be territorialized according to various levels of organization (being-animal, beinghuman, being-woman, being-male, and the most totalizing of all, Law, or, beingman)[19], but the priority of the joining of beings in a universal language of finitude is an always already present condition through which beings speak. Appropriating and overturning Heidegger's phraseology: there is no Being, like the *Mitsein* of animals, where language speaks the limit of 'man.'

Deleuze and Guattari's work represents a major attempt to think the joining of beings beyond that which we normally think in terms of language. "Language" in their work constitutes communicative sharings (or "communities") which are not limited either by categories of the understanding or by explicit experiences of finitude. Their work allows a radical rereading of finitude away from science, and of informational lines away from systems, including systems of understanding. They allow us to read human finitude in terms of a universal joining, rather than as the limit of that joining. In short, they allow a reading of "community" even beyond the limitations of a Heideggerian vocabulary and allow us to think information and the limit on a universal scale without closure. That is, to think "community" according to a *universal* scale of what Nancy has termed "infinite finitude."

Conclusion

Contrary to the current ideology of the 'information community,' that which still occurs within a rational community to-come, an immanence which is achievable either by a teleological or Christian sense of totality, or by a democratic mythos of equally recognized voices regulated within a strict economy of rational form, the problematic of translation introduces a notion of information as in-form-ing. That is, *the thinking through of translation is the thinking through of the in-forming action of information, and is a deterritorialization of positive notions of information.* In translation, formation and trans-formation are not to be forgotten.

Information in the post-apocalyptical community is not virtual, in the sense of a rational community that has been lost and will be found again in each voice expressing its 'true' self, but rather, in the abandonment of such ideals that regulate the rationality of modernity, information's relation to community is that of the appearance of what Nancy and Agamben refer to as 'singularity' as it founds community. As Agamben argues though, the community founded upon the authenticity of each regardless of a governing principle of utopia-to-come stands the chance of an utmost dissolution into bourgeois boredom, and the Law utterly unclothed as the en-framing (Heidegger, *Ge-stell*) of, and for, market capitalism, with its *false concern*, its *lying 'care' for* the 'whole,' now on a transnational scale; a 'concern' which runs completely *counter* to the very premises, goals, and history of capitalism. We already witness a smooth replacement of one center by another in the transition from the household's Law to the universalism of the media; from the repressive, and even difficult, *heimlich* superego, to the omnipotent *unheimlich* voice of truth that can never be ritualistically killed, and which is literally unanswerable. On the other hand, the very exhaustiveness of this voice of repetition, its already too massive scale, and its necessary silence regarding any actual community, causes a chasm to occur in the mythos of the democratic *polis* which coincides, and repeats, the collapse of modernism's universal narratives. As Nancy argues,

> We do not know it, we cannot really know it, but abandoned being has already begun to constitute an inevitable condition for our thought, perhaps its only condition. From now on, the ontology that summons us will be an ontology in which abandonment remains the sole predicament of being, in which it even remains—in the scholastic sense of the word—the transcendental. If being has not ceased to speak itself in multiple *ways—pollakos legetai—abandonment* adds nothing to the proliferation of this *pollakos*. It sums up the proliferation, assembles it, but by exhausting it, carrying it to the extreme poverty of abandonment. Being speaks itself as abandoned by all categories, all transcendentals. Abandoned being immobilizes the *dialectic* whose name means "the one that abandons nothing, ever,

> the one that endlessly joins, resumes, recovers." It obstructs or forsakes the very position, the initial position, of being.
>
> ("Abandoned Being," 36-37)

Abandoned being is read by humanism as the utmost sign of nihilism, because with its abandonment enlightenment is lost. But it is this very abandonment which Kierkegaard favors in arguing against dialectic in the singular individual's im-possible move in faith, a faith gained by a singular repetition when faced with the impossible. Such moments of continual rebirths of the world, of authentic repetition, are given the name in Heidegger's writings of *"Wiederholung,"* which summons the sense of a retrieval that repeats while marking difference. What is communicated here is the communication of that Being which includes alterity.

An "in-formed" Being is a being which is always already in the past, in a discursive formation of being-told. Even in the 'findings' of information, such as with evidence, information does not shout out its meaning, evidence does not 'speak for itself.' Such self-deception in regard to the meaning of information allows one to flow as 'one' within a discursive surface or series of surfaces, systemically arranged. Some may argue that this is the 'pragmatic' nature of information. But the *pragma*, the affairs or circumstances of information, involve the in-forming of things through language. Replying to the *pragma* of information means critically translating rhetorical surfaces according to the demands of finitude, of historicity, and extension.

As Agamben has argued, it is through language that singularity figures itself. But is also through the process of trans-figuration that language is thrown into a future and a past made possible by singularity itself. The transfiguration of singularity by means of translation transforms the figure of singularity even as it transforms the figuration and figurability of language. The essence of this circle of transformation between the figure of singularity and the tone of language is the in-forming of language and finitude by each other. Such in-forming is the ground upon which community is founded in the act of dialogue and the sharing of language.

By no means can the 'animal' be discounted from such in-forming. Though Hölderlin is correct to speak of the "figure of man" as that which most expresses "man," the abandonment of Being means an expansion of ontology beyond itself, and ultimately, an abandonment of ontology and even the question of man. Abandonment as the basis for community must abandon itself when faced with the question of the animal. Because it is at such a point that the circle of temporality which propels man and language faces a mode of Being that is both more proper to human being, and yet, is said to be most alien. Human being as animal-becomings must come to terms with senses that stand beyond the central problems of ontology. Translation, though without the apocalypse of transfiguration, continues, despite the absence of a monumental figure. The community of the animal, a community that we may speak of in terms of sense, is a community of translation without monumental transfigurations (though we cannot doubt that transfiguration does occur, for example, in the Law which arises between one's pets and the pet's humans). The nature of singularity in regard to the animal is devoid of all liberal 'rights,' but it demands utmost regard to finitude and specificity at each and every moment. Its demands cannot be recuperated in terms of 'one' or the 'other' but must be in regard to an all without capital, without reifying such and such being, but in full attention to the specificity of contact.

The line or trace of information thus extends beyond the possibility of any system or modality. Today, the ethical demand is the unforgetting of infinite finitude.

Endnotes

1. See Samuel Weber's "The Vaulted Eye: Remarks on Knowledge and Professionalism" and "The Limits of Professionalism" for arguments and critiques linking professionalization and the construction of the sciences.

2. Martin Heidegger discusses the importance of the "what" in relation to the sciences and philosophy in the beginning of "What is Metaphysics?"

3. See Berman, chapter 1.

4. See "Roundtable on Translation," 102. Also, Derrida's "Me Psychoanalysis: An Introduction to the Translation of 'The Shell and the Kernel' by Nicolas Abraham."

5. Maurice Blanchot, "The Most Profound Question," *The Infinite Conversation*, 20.

6. This paper, itself, may be read in terms of a translation of "information" according to a philosophy that has been deterritorialized by an encounter with the poetic (that is, in terms of a post-modern philosophy, or a philosophy at the "end of philosophy, the beginning of thinking" (Heidegger)). The "end of philosophy"—an end marked by the unforgetting of philosophy's restrictive repetitions and metaphors (not only in, and as, philosophy as a discipline, but in terms of science and representative identity)—not by an end to its general economy of repetition—would, in fact, announce a critique of "information," as such a term would fall under a critique of philosophy's critical self-(dis)closure).

7. See Derrida's *Of Grammatology* for a reading of "*différance*" in terms of the oppositions between writing and speech (as presence) in the Western philosophical tradition.

8. For example, from the translator's notes to "Des Tours de Babel" (Joseph F. Graham):

> "Des Tours de Babel." The title can be read in various ways. Des means 'some'; but it also means 'of the,' 'from the,' or 'about the.' Tours could be towers, twists, tricks, turns, or tropes, as in a "turn" of phrase. Taken together, des and tours have the same sound as detour, the word for detour. To mark that economy in language the title has not been changed. (206)

9. For an excellent reading of this problem, see Fritz Gutbrodt, "Poedelaire: Translation and the Volatility of the Letter" (*Diacritics*, fall/winter, 1992).

10. See Berman, chapter 3.

11. See chapter 4 of Berman's *The Experience of the Foreign*.

12. See Fritz Machlup, "Semantic Quirks in Studies of Information," and Fritz Machlup and Una Mansfield, "Cultural Diversity in studies of Information," in *The Study of Information: Interdisciplinary Messages*.

13. On this, see particularly, Philippe Lacoue-Labarthe's *Heidegger, Art, and Politics*.

14. See Agamben's *The Coming Community* for a discussion of "such." Heesok Chang's review of this text in *Postmodern Culture*, v.4 n.1, accurately stresses that the "such" is to be understood in Agamben's text in terms of the singularity, and the term "exposure" be thought, following Nancy and Heidegger, in terms of the singularity's experience of finitude and the failure of identity to exhaust this experience. I would also like to open up a different sense of "such" and "exposure" by stressing the role of "as" in the determination of "such" in its exposure. "Exposure" can be thought, as Agamben notes elsewhere in the text, in terms of image. Thus, the exposure of such cannot only be thought in terms of its appearance in the open of Being, but in terms of its encounter against what Deleuze and Guattari term "surfaces" of meaning. Such a thinking of "such" in terms of its being "such and such" would be, in Heidegger's terminology, an ontic rather than an ontological determination of the "such" and of "exposure," but I think the term "exposure" demands that we think both the "as" in terms of a difference intrinsic to its metaphoricity and in terms of its closure as the "exposure" of a singularity in contact with in-formed surfaces of meaning. Indeed, the limit experience which Nancy et. al. attempt to keep before us occurs at the limit of such surfaces, and such limitation allows the occurrence of art as both a tracing of the limit and as a pressing of the problem of measure (the problem of the stability of surface) through art. The "exposure" of the artist in terms of the surface 'under critique,' sort of speaking, is a problem of reducing "exposure" in the sense Nancy offers it with "exposure" in terms of the identification imposed by the surface. Such "exposure" forms, however, part of the event of the work, and cannot be avoided.

    To put it in a broader language: the "such" is not reducible to identity, but on the other hand, the thinking of "such" cannot avoid its exposure as such-and-such an identity. The plurality of identities, even in a singular identity ("such and such"), constitutes the dissemination of anything, as such—a dissem(e)-ination which Derrida makes much of in, among other works, "Des Tours de Babel."

15. See for example, Derrida's comments in *Of Spirit*, as well as his important remarks in Jean-Luc Nancy's interview entitled, "'Eating Well': An Interview." Among his remarks, we excerpt the following:

    > The Heideggerian discourse on the animal is violent and awkward, at times contradictory. Heidegger does not simply say "The animal is poor in world [*weltarm*]," for, as distinct from the stone, it has a world. He says: the animal *has* a world in the mode of a *nothaving*. But this not-having does not constitute in his view an indigence, the *lack* of a world that would be human. So why this negative determination? Where does it come from? There is no *category* [my italics (RD): what is evident here is the problem of thinking the animal outside of categories of the understanding] of original existence for

> the animal: it is evidently not *Dasein*, either as *vorhandene* or *zuhandene* (Being cannot appear, be, or be questioned as such [*als*] for the animal. It's simple existence introduces a principle of disorder or of limitation into the conceptuality of *Being and Time*. (111)
>
> Discourses as original as those of Heidegger and Levinas disrupt, of course, a certain traditional humanism. In spite of the differences separating them, they nonetheless remain profound humanisms to *the extent that they do not sacrifice sacrifice*. The subject (in Levinas's sense) and the *Dasein* are "men" in a world where sacrifice is possible and where it is not forbidden to make an attempt on life in general, but only on the life of a man, of other kin, on the other as *Dasein*. Heidegger does not say it this way.
>
> But what he places at the origin of moral conscience (or rather *Gewissen*) is obviously denied to the animal. *Mitsein* is not conferred, if we can say so, on the living in general, no more than is *Dasein*, but only on that being-toward-death that also makes the *Dasein* into something else, something more and better than a living [thing]." (113)

My remarks in what follow continue along these lines, and even as they, perhaps overboldly and to some extent incautiously, critique the limits of Nancy and Derrida's works (among others) on the "question of the animal," they fully are indebted to these writers' depth of thinking on the subject as, I hope, the above quotations demonstrate.

16. See Jacques Derrida, "Freud and the Scene of Writing," in *Writing and Difference*.

17. This can be expressed variously as the fact that the phallus is not equivalent to the penis in Lacanian psychoanalysis, or in Deleuze and Guattari's writing, that the "zones" of 'majority,' however they may be constituted ('man,' 'rational' (i.e., not animal), 'white,' etc.) are zones which may be occupied by anyone, regardless of metaphysically categorized self-identities (self-identities based in categorical group identification). Such zones are characterized by stasis, a resistance to becoming and to sliding into other zones, and are essentially repressive (Deleuze and Guattari argue, for example, that all other becomings (e.g., becomings animals) must begin with becoming-woman, that is, for human beings, the movement away from the repressiveness of a central point and history). Deleuze and Guattari's diagram in footnote 82 in chapter 4 shows this quite well. They argue this schema as the "arborescent schema of majority" according to the "subordination of the line to the point" (544). The depiction of the "line" follows their notion of "rhizome" as movements of becoming according to the proximity of zones of 'being' (loosely, not categorically, understood) in relation to one another. I take solid lines in the diagrams to indicate normative returns to "man" (for the male, through the experience of the woman, and for the adult, through the experience of the child—these routes, by the way, would duplicate the traditional psychoanalytical models of

development for men and adults in general). Broken lines would indicate 'abnormal' lines of development (note that they would circulate as exterior to the return to 'man,' and they would embody all four points. Deleuze and Guattari seem to indicate, in the main text, that this circulation would come to constitute 'minority' histories, etc.: "Of course, the child, the woman, the black have memories; but the Memory that collects those memories is still a virile majoritarian agency treating them as 'childhood memories,' as conjugal or colonial memories" (293).

18. Benjamin argues this ideal "expression" of the masses in the state as the "aestheticization of politics" ("The Work of Art in the Mechanical Age of Reproduction," *Illuminations*, 241). In light of our former chapter, we may remember that Benjamin reads such "expression" within fascism as the *full* utilization of technical resources to their fullest expression (an expression which, Benjamin argues, can only be accomplished in the form of war, and which presupposes, a maintenance of property relations, that is, a resistance to redistributing excess resources created by unemployment and the lack of markets (242)). The line blurs between mechanical and human resources once the latter have been defined in terms of normativity and absolute reproduction (i.e., in terms of the absolute, that is, traditionally, 'man' (and within the mimetic tradition, 'state')), and have come to see their means of production as a cultural production. The expression of a "national culture" can thus occur through the means of technical machinery: for example, through the use of bombs or through the installment of machinery that promotes the communicative rhetoric which defines and preserves that home culture. The promotion of information technology upon postcolonial countries can be read, from this angle, as a continuation of the "cold war's" attempt to realign these countries with Western capital markets by an aesthetic mixture of mechanical form and political function. A 'new world order' of virtual communication—that is, linguistic and cultural containment—which in truth begins before the Second World War and continues today.

19. "Man constitutes himself as a gigantic memory, through the position of the central point, its frequency (insofar as it is necessarily reproduced by each dominant point), and its resonance (insofar as all of the points tie in with it" (and ff.) (*A Thousand Plateaus*, 293).

See also the third endnote of this chapter, above.

Bibliography

Abraham, N. & N. Rand. "The Shell and the Kernel." *Diacritics*, 9(1), 1979. 16–28.

Agamben. G. *The Coming Community*. Trans. M. Hardt. University of Minnesota Press, 1993.

Benjamin, W. "The Task of the Translator." *Illuminations*. Ed. H. Arendt. Harcourt, Brace, & World, 1985. 69–82.

Benjamin, W. "The Work of Art in the Age of Mechanical Reproduction." *Illuminations*. Ed. H. Arendt. Harcourt, Brace, & World, 1985. 217–51.

Berman, A. *The Experience of the Foreign*. Trans. S. Heyvaert. SUNY Press, 1992.

Blanchot, M. "The Most Profound Question." *The Infinite Conversation*. Trans. S. Hanson. University of Minnesota Press, 1993. 11–24.

Cesareo, G. "Towards An Electronic Democracy?" *The Critical Communication Review*, 2, 1983. 71–84.

Deleuze, G. & F. Guattari. *A Thousand Plateaus: Capitalism and Schizophrenia*. Trans. B. Massumi. University of Minnesota Press, 1987.

Derrida, J. "Des Tours de Babel." Trans. J. F. Graham. *Difference in Translation*. Cornell University Press, 1985. 165–248.

Derrida, J. "Me-Psychoanalysis: An Introduction to the Translation of 'The Shell and the Kernel' by Nicolas Abraham." Trans. R. Klein. *Diacritics*, March 1979. 4-12.

Derrida, J. *The Other Heading: Reflections on Today's Europe*. Trans. P-A. Brault & M. B. Naas. Indiana University Press, 1992.

Derrida, J. "Roundtable on Translation." *The Ear of the Other: Otobiography, Transference, Translation*. Ed. C. V. McDonald. Trans. P. Kamuf. Schocken Books, 1985.

Gutbrodt, F. "Poedelaire: Translation and the Volatility of the Letter." *Diacritics*, Fall/Winter, 1992. 49-68.

Heidegger, M. *Being and Time*. Trans. J. Macquarrie & E. Robinson. Harper and Row, 1962.

Heidegger, M. *The Concept of Time*. Trans. W. McNeil. Blackwell, 1992.

Heidegger, M. "What is Metaphysics?" Trans. D. F. Krell. *Basic Writings*. Ed. D. F. Krell. Harper and Row, 1977. 91–112.

Lacoue-Labarthe, P. *Heidegger, Art, and Politics*. Trans. C. Turner. Basil Blackwell, 1990.

Machlup, F. "Semantic Quirks in Studies of Information." *The Study of Information: Interdisciplinary Messages*. Ed. F. Machlup & U. Mansfield. John Wiley and Sons, 1983. 641–72.

Machlup, F. & U. Mansfield. "Cultural Diversity in Studies of Information." *The Study of Information: Interdisciplinary Messages*. Ed. F. Machlup & U. Mansfield. John Wiley and Sons, 1983. 3-56.

Nancy, J.-L. "Beheaded Sun (*Soleil cou coupé*)." Trans. B. Gold & B. Holmes. *Qui Parle*, 3(2), Fall 1989. 40-53.

Nancy, J.-L. "Abandoned Being." Trans. B. Holmes. *The Birth to Presence*. Stanford University Press, 1993. 36-47.

Nancy, J.-L. "'Eating Well,' or the Calculation of the Subject: An Interview with Jacques Derrida." Trans. P. Connor & A. Ronell. *Who Comes After the Subject?* Ed. E. Cadava, P. Connor, J-L. Nancy. Routledge, 1991.

Nancy, J.-L. "The Inoperative Community." Trans. P. Connor. *The Inoperative Community*. Ed. P. Connor. University of Minnesota, 1991. 1-42.

Nancy, J.-L. "Sharing Voices." Trans. G. L. Ormiston. *Transforming the Hermeneutic Context: From Nietzsche to Nancy*. Eds. G. L. Ormiston & A. D. Schrift. SUNY Press, 1990. 211-259.

Saussure, F. D. *Course in General Linguistics*. Columbia University Press, 2011.

Weber, S. "The Limits of Professionalism" *Oxford Literary Review*, 5(1), 1982. 59-79.

Weber, S. "The Vaulted Eye: Remarks on Knowledge and Professionalism." *Reading the Archives: On Texts and Institutions* (Yale French Studies, 77 (1990)). 44- 60.

Wittgenstein, L. *Philosophical Investigations*. Basil Blackwell, 1976.

Index

AI. *See* artificial intelligence
ALISE. *See* Association for Library and Information Science Education
American Society for Information Science, 1-2, 9
animal songs, 13-14
artificial intelligence, 5
ASIS. *See* American Society for Information Science
ASIS&T. *See* Association for Information Science and Technology
Association for Information Science and Technology, 1-2
Association for Library and Information Science Education, 4
autonomous movement, 7, 10

bibliography, 8, 17, 18-19, 32, 43, 45
Braman, Sandra, 3-4
Briet, Suzanne, 1-2
British Classification Research Group, 8
Buckland, Michael, 1-2, 5, 12

capitalism, 77-80
classification, faceted, 23, 26-27
classification, library, 9, 21, 24
classification, natural science, 9
classification, zoological, 9
Classification Research Group, 5, 26-28
classification theory, 17, 19-20, 26, 43-45
communication, 3, 11, 12, 23-26, 61, 86-87
community, 6, 10, 60, 75-76, 85, 87-88, 90-91, 95
Computer Professionals for Social Responsibility, 3
Cooper, Robert, 8-9
CPSR. *See* Computer Professionals for Social Responsibility
CRG. *See* Classification Research Group
critical information studies, 4, 9
critical librarianship. *See* librarianship, critical
critical poetics, 3-4
critical study, 62
cultural theory, 3, 61
cybernetics, 5, 6, 8, 17, 18, 39-40, 42, 60

Day, Ronald E., 1, 3-4, 8-9, 10-12
Deleuze, Gilles, 2
democracy, 72-73, 76-77, 81
Drucker, Johanna, 3

faceted classification. *See* classification, faceted
fascism, 6, 7, 69, 75, 81, 94
Fremery, Wayne de, 3, 9-10

Genz, Marcella, 2

Hahn, Trudi Bellardo, 1-2
Heidegger, Martin, 2, 3, 10, 11, 13, 18
human rights, 85-86

identity, 7, 21, 69-72, 80
in-between, 7-8, 13, 62
in-formation, 7-8, 11, 13-14, 36
individuality, 7, 14, 82, 85
information
  algorithmic weighting of, 5
  as affective attunements, 11
  as differential affects in documentation systems, 11
  as epistemic substance, 2, 6
  as flow, 60
  as knowledge, 2
  as process, 2
  as relation, 7
  as substance, 7
  as thing, 2
  auto-affective presence of, 2-3, 6
  blurring of, 34
  conceptual meaning of, 1
  conduit metaphor for, 3, 5, 10, 23-24, 61
  critique of, 4
  cultural power of, 1
  definitions of, 1, 2, 6, 31, 60, 73
  deterritorialized readings of, 60
  discursive aspects of, 4, 60
  from historical perspective, 1, 17
  from philosophical perspective, 17
  global aspect of, 81-82
  historiography of, 2, 62
  modern conception of, 2, 6, 11
  modes of 97

phenomenology of, 2
raw data as, 6
relation to alterity, 60-61
seeker of, 5
situational nature of, 24
user of, 5
information age, 2-3, 33, 77
information society, 3, 6, 11
information systems, 5, 10, 25, 31, 43
information technology, 3, 63, 76-78
informational capitalism, 6
inter-zone, 97-100

Josiah Macy Jr. Foundation, 8

Keele University Center for the Social Studies of Technology, 8-9
Keele University CSST. *See* Keele University Center for the Social Studies of Technology
knowledge
  blurring of, 34
  classification schemata of, 19-22, 27, 43
  consumption of, 25-26
  critique of, 4
  nature of, 18
  situational nature of, 24
  transmission of, 17, 23
  universe of, 21, 22

Lakoff, George, 4
language, 6, 7, 24, 35-36, 73-75, 80, 82-84, 86, 89, 91-93, 100
Language Poetry/Language Writing movement, 3, 4
Larson, Ray, 1, 5, 8
Latour, Bruno, 12
librarianship, critical, 12
librarianship, whole person, 12
library and information science
  computationally oriented aspect of, 1
  doctoral level education in, 1, 12
  focus on information in, 1
  fundamental issues in, 45
  history of, 1, 3, 8
  i-school movement in, 3, 12
  literature of, 2, 17, 19
  master level education in, 1, 12
library classification. *See* classification, library
LIS. *See* library and information science

machine learning, 5
Macy Conference on Cybernetics, 5
Marxism, 2, 9
metaphors, 9-10, 17-20, 29, 43, 60
metaphysical presence, 2, 6, 11, 25, 39, 43
modernism, 33, 34-35, 36-37, 43, 63, 81

natural science classification. *See* classification, natural science
neoliberalism, 6, 8
neural networks, 5

Otlet, Paul, 1-2

poetry, 66, 71-72
post-structuralism, 2, 3, 8
pragmatics, 31, 35, 61-63, 91-92, 102
PRECIS. *See* Preserved Context Index System
Preserved Context Index System, 26-27

Ranganathan, S. R., 21-27, 44
Rayward, W. Boyd, 1-2
romanticism, 43

singularity, 6-7, 14, 82, 101, 102-103
small presses, 3-4
subjectivity, 5, 33, 34, 43-44
systems, 8, 17, 29-30, 32, 36, 43-45
systems theory, 11, 17, 25, 28-33, 43-45

technology, 3, 12, 18, 37, 60
time, 10, 23, 24-25, 29, 36-42
translation, 6, 63-69, 71-72, 77

whole person librarianship. *See* librarianship, whole person
Williams, Robert, 1-2
Wilson, Patrick, 1
Woolf, Douglas, 3-4
World Wide Web, 10
WWW. *See* World Wide Web

zoological classification. *See* classification, zoological

www.ingramcontent.com/pod-product-compliance
Lightning Source LLC
Chambersburg PA
CBHW052052220426
43663CB00012B/2545